Mafia Democracy

Mafia Democracy

HOW OUR REPUBLIC

BECAME A MOB RACKET

Michael Franzese

LIONCREST
PUBLISHING

MAFIA DEMOCRACY

How Our Republic Became a Mob Racket

FIRST EDITION

ISBN   978-1-5445-3082-6 *Hardcover*
      978-1-5445-3081-9 *Paperback*
      978-1-5445-3080-2 *Ebook*
      978-1-5445-3083-3 *Audiobook*

This book is dedicated to all you honest, hard working American citizens, as well as to your sons, daughters, grandchildren, and future generations. It's dedicated to the men and women of our military who give their lives to defend the freedom of the United States of America. To the law enforcement officers who preserve the order fairly and ethically. To the fair-minded and upright elected officials who uphold the Constitution. To all who honor and respect the America our forefathers envisioned some 250 years ago. And to the God I serve and ask in daily prayer to Bless America.

Contents

Foreword

By Rudy Giuliani

IF YOU HAD TOLD ME IN 1985 THAT I WOULD WRITE A foreword for a book by an ex-Mafia caporegime, I would have laughed you out of my office. Thirty-seven years ago, I was putting Mob bosses behind bars, not helping them get their stories out to the public.

But here I am.

Although I had a reputation as a relentless federal prosecutor of the American and Sicilian Mafia, Wall Street fraudsters, Nazis, Colombian cartels and the FARC, terrorism, and corrupt Republicans and Democrats, I never lost my firm belief in redemption. It is true that recidivism is the rule, and redemption is often feigned, but there is embedded in the human personality the desire to do good.

Two thousand years ago, an overzealous Jewish-Roman citizen made his reputation as the most fearsome and effective pursuer and assassin of early Christians. His cruel excessive use of torture and murder was driven by the same motivation as that of Eastern Europeans who ran concentration camps and slaughtered thousands of Jews and Orthodox to gain preferment within the Third Reich and promotion in the SS. Paul even personally supervised the stoning of St. Stephen. And then on the road to Damascus he was confronted with his atrocities by the intervention of Christ Jesus and became even more dedicated and zealous and effective in spreading the word of the Lord through Eastern Europe and Asia Minor.

Redemption is the work of the Lord.

Let me tell you why I'm writing this foreword for Michael Franzese.

I first met Michael when my team was prosecuting him. Michael was among the various Mob guys I went after in the mid-1980s when I was the US Attorney for the Southern District of New York. Our biggest case during that period was the 1985–86 Mafia Commission Trial, where we took on the Five Families of New York's Mafia and won. *Time* magazine called it the "Case of Cases," and we sent the likes of Tony Salerno, Carmine Persico, and the heads of the Five Families to prison with one-hundred-year sentences. We also sent two hundred of their members and eight hundred of their Sicilian co-conspirators to prison for all or most of the remainder of their lives. A few, like Paul Castellano and Thomas Bilotti, were murdered by their own.

I came to know Michael Franzese during those years. He was a high-profile figure in the Colombo crime family, and his father, Sonny Franzese, was a long-time Mafia boss before going to prison for fifty years. We prosecuted Michael more than once in those years and were never able to get a conviction. But I knew it was just a matter of time.

I remember attending one of his trials during this period. Michael was at the defense table with his lawyer, and I was chatting with my prosecutors handling the case. Someone later recalled how I turned to address Michael's attorney. "His father is in prison for fifty years," I said, nodding in Michael's direction. "But we're going to put his son in prison for a hundred years!" I spoke loud enough for Michael to hear.

Michael had his hand in a lot of different schemes, but by far the biggest one was his lucrative scam to cheat the government out of gas taxes. Through an elaborate daisy chain network, Michael and his crew used eighteen stock-bearer companies based in Panama to defraud the government out of these taxes, pocketing as much as $8 million a week.

We later estimated that the scam cost New York over $250 million in stolen gas taxes. Florida may have lost nearly that much when Michael expanded to the south. Meanwhile, the "Yuppie Don," as Michael was called in the newspapers, became something of a media darling. He was listed at number eighteen on *Fortune* magazine's list of the "Fifty Most Wealthy and Powerful Mob Bosses," and *Vanity Fair* claimed he was the biggest moneymaker in the Mafia since Al Capone. I have to admit that seeing these articles angered me and made me even more determined to send this "Prince of the Mafia" to prison for a long time.

In March 1985, we struck a deal that would allow Michael to plead guilty to racketeering conspiracy and tax conspiracy. He was sentenced to ten years in prison and agreed to pay $15 million in restitution. This settlement was a significant piece of our success in crippling the organized crime network in New York City.

In subsequent years, I got into politics and was elected mayor of New York City in 1993. I served two terms. I helped clean up the city and return it to its former glory, and after 9/11, I helped unite the city during our greatest crisis. During these years, I'd hear about Michael Franzese from time to time. Someone told me he'd left the Mafia. At first I was skeptical—the Mafia isn't a social club that allows its members to just leave—but as time went on I could see additional evidence that Michael had turned his life around. He had shifted his attention to lifting people up rather than controlling or intimidating them in the way of Mob bosses. As time went by and the conversion remained constant, I was impressed by how he had publicly left a life of crime.

Over the years, I heard more and more about Michael. He wrote books and traveled the country giving speeches. He became a devout Christian. More than a few people told me that I should listen to what he had to say about politics. I'm a conservative Republican, and Michael, I learned, shared many of my beliefs and attitudes.

In 2021, I was invited to be on a podcast with Michael hosted by my friend Joe Pagliarulo. I didn't hesitate to accept. "How's Michael doing?" I asked Pags, a mutual friend.

What Michael did with his life was not easy. I'd seen too many criminals go to jail and come out and start breaking the law all over again. But Michael had been sincere and forthright. He spoke in a way that was more powerful and compelling. As I said, I truly believe in, and respect, redemption. It was clear to me that Michael had redeemed himself.

Meeting with Michael that day confirmed for me that I had been correct about him. I had read a lot of his writing, watched him on television, and saw how he had developed. I had an instinct that he was legitimate, and I found myself thinking, "This is what can happen to human beings. You *can* change. You *can* put your past behind you and become a better person." I believe as a Catholic and as a Christian that it is the work of the Holy Spirit reaching the goodness placed there by our Creator.

God has different directions for us, and I can see that he set Michael on a fresh, new direction. Michael broke the law and went to prison, but he came out a different and better person. And just as he was helped through that transition, he now works to help others.

Understand this as you read through this book. Michael cares about this country and he cares about its citizens. He wants us to have a strong country, and he feels we deserve the best, most honest politicians we can elect. The fact that he doesn't see that happening today is troubling to him, and he's willing to use his notoriety and his large following to set things right.

Understand also that Michael's view of politics comes from a perspective that few people get to have. He's seen what the criminal life is like, and he knows how criminals victimize those around them. So when Michael sees this behavior in our elective officials, he feels compelled to point out what's happening and attempt to stop it.

Let's join him in that effort. Our political system is struggling today for many of the reasons Michael examines in this book. Let's all become aware of those problems and work to solve them. Change is not going to happen overnight and it's going to take more than one book to change what's happening. But, armed with the knowledge Michael imparts in this book, we have the fodder we need to fight back.

Introduction

"Liberty cannot be preserved without a general knowledge among the people, who have a right...and a desire to know."

—JOHN ADAMS, 1765

YOU COULD SAY JOHN MURTHA WAS AN AMERICAN HERO. He served with distinction in the Marines in the 1950s and then ten years later volunteered for the Vietnam War, where he earned two Purple Hearts and a Bronze Star. In 1974, the former Eagle Scout was elected to Congress and became the longest-serving congressman in Pennsylvania history. He lived modestly. He owned a small car wash in Johnstown. He was regarded as a fierce defender and protector of his district, which had been decimated by the decline of the coal and steel industries.

When he died in 2010 at age seventy-seven, Defense Secretary Robert M. Gates called Murtha "a true patriot." Murtha was, in every respect, the antithesis of a made man in the Mafia. Or was he really?

Murtha was the ranking Democrat on the Appropriation

Committee's military subcommittee. This gave him a lot of clout. Like a Mafia capo in charge of a crew that earns big dollars for the family. Over the years, Murtha figured out how to funnel federal dollars not only to his home state but also to his relatives, former colleagues, and business associates. Sound familiar, President Biden? In the Mafia, this kind of diversion of money gets you killed. In government, diverting taxpayer money to outside sources provides the perpetrator with big benefits. As the Mafia boss Carlo Gambino once said, "Judges, lawyers, and politicians have a license to steal. We don't need one." I'm not saying Murtha slipped our federal tax dollars into his own pockets, but his deal-making and control over appropriation earmarks made him a lot of friends. He rarely had trouble getting reelected, and his campaign coffers were always brimming with donations from grateful constituents.

Although his first campaign slogan was "One Honest Man is Enough," Murtha used his power in Congress to pass out checks like a rich uncle at Christmas. In the 1980s, Murtha was nearly ensnared in an FBI sting operation when he was videotaped discussing payoffs from a federal agent posing as a sheik seeking favors. Years later, a lobbying firm Murtha worked with was raided by federal agents who were investigating improper campaign contributions. Another lobbying firm paid for a driver for Murtha, and a principal in that firm—a former appropriations staffer who worked with Murtha—was later sent to jail for two years for improper campaign contributions. In 2007, the Justice Department began investigating why Murtha was directing earmarks to clients of his brother Robert's "consulting" firm. The feds were particularly interested in earmark recipients who had no offices, websites, or phone numbers, appeared to do little work, and were owned by principals at the lobbying firm.

Murtha's activities were one of the worst-kept secrets on

Capitol Hill. No one blew the whistle because few dared to challenge Murtha for fear he would cut them out of the appropriations process altogether. In Congress, that's known as power. But extortion is a better term for that kind of retaliation.

The Price of Power

My point here isn't that Murtha was a remarkably deceitful politician. My point is that Murtha's behavior is standard practice today in American politics. Politicians like Murtha leave for Washington as members of the middle class and return home millionaires. They enrich themselves through earmarks, grants, and regulations that benefit their family members and associates. They serve a few terms doing the bidding of powerful industry lobbyists, and then they leave office for high-paying jobs with the very same firms they previously regulated.

It's nice work if you can get it.

But most politicians don't have to leave office to get rich. Mitch McConnell, the Republican from Kentucky, has quadrupled his wealth since being elected. The key words being "since being elected." He's worth around $12 million, although his Senate salary is only $174,000 a year.

Nancy Pelosi was already well off when she was first elected to Congress but has managed to get even wealthier using her office. For instance, she secured nearly $1 billion for a light rail project that also happened to increase the value of a San Francisco office building she owns by an estimated 150 percent. She's also directed earmarks to waterfront redevelopment and beautification projects adjacent to other properties she owns. In 2010, she helped Rep. Bernie Thompson, a Democrat from Michigan, become chair of the powerful House Homeland Security Committee. That same year, Thompson got an earmark to upgrade the Napa Valley airport near other properties Pelosi and her husband own. All this time, Pelosi has hypocritically vowed to root out corruption on Capitol Hill. "What we have to do is drain the swamp in Washington, DC," she said in 2006. I guess she meant every swamp but her own.

Harry Reid got $18 million to build a bridge no one wanted— except Reid himself, who happened to own land near the bridge. (Harry was a friend to the Mob going way back.) Former House Speaker Dennis Hastert made millions by buying some land in Illinois and then finding federal money to build a highway next to it. Finding "federal money" typically means using your tax dollars for pet projects that will line their pockets.

Like most concerned Americans, I've watched these shenanigans from a distance for many years. But unlike most citizens, I can see our elected officials' behavior for what it really is—a Mafia-style Democracy. Our elected leaders have become racketeers proficient in carrying out Mob-like rackets, and we are all suffering as a result. They are getting rich as they exert increasing control over our lives.

This is how the Mafia operates too. It's all about control.

I can say this because from the mid-1970s to the mid-1990s, I was a made member of the Colombo crime family in New York City. I started out as a soldier and eventually became a *caporegime* with a crew of nearly three hundred made men and associates. I was known as an "earner" because I developed illegal schemes that made the family millions of dollars each week.

During my years in the Mafia, a.k.a. Cosa Nostra in America, we infiltrated almost every major industry in America. We controlled the unions, the construction sites, and the shipyards. We bribed judges, city and state officials, and local cops. We created "associations" to control the cost of garbage collection. We controlled gambling and the numbers. We bribed athletes to shave points so we could maximize our gambling profits. We shylocked, and when businesses couldn't repay our exorbitant interest rates, we took over their operations and pocketed their earnings. We controlled all of the concrete contractors in the city, taking a percentage off every cubic foot of concrete poured for big developers like Jerry Gutterman, Harry Helmsley, and Donald Trump. We extracted kickbacks from contractors putting up police stations and prisons.

I left that life in 1995. After serving almost eight years in prison on racketeering conspiracy and tax charges, I decided my life as a gangster/racketeer was over and that I needed to walk away. By then, the Mob in New York was a shadow of its former self. The feds had put away most of the crime family bosses, and made men and associates were testifying against the Mob to avoid long prison terms. Federal agents had legal wiretaps everywhere. The life we knew was over. So I quit and moved to California with my wife, Camille, and our children and never looked back. I did look over my shoulder from time to time—both the government and the media say I am the only capo to ever publicly walk away from the Mafia, not enter a witness protection program, and go on to lead a fairly normal life with my family—but I've never testified against any of my former Mob associates nor did I do anything or reveal anything to law enforcement to cause any former associate to spend even a day in prison. Although I was very aware that leaving the Mafia could have resulted in severe consequences, I do not live in fear for my life.

But I do fear for the future of my children and grandchildren, who are currently living in a land governed by all too many corrupt politicians. And that's why I'm writing this book.

How the Mob Rule

When you're a "made man," it is almost inevitable that you will end up in prison at some point. That happens when you're engaged in criminal activities. And when you do, it's almost required that you read a copy of *The Prince* by Machiavelli. So that's what I did.

Niccolò Machiavelli is considered by many to be the father of modern political science. He was a writer and a diplomat in sixteenth-century Italy, and his name has become synonymous with deceit.

In *The Prince*, he recommends that leaders embrace immoral behavior—including violence and deception—to maintain power. A leader must appear to be virtuous, but to maintain power, the leader sometimes has to lie, steal, and cheat, Machiavelli said. You must do whatever it takes to maintain control of your kingdom. Machiavelli's theory was the guiding philosophy for the Mafia. You must appear to be honest and respectful, but you can't let morals and ethical behavior undercut your power. Power, control, and influence are everything to a made man.

In the years after I got out of prison and walked away from the Mafia, I wrote books, consulted for businesses, and gave public talks about my life and the power of my faith in God. I also watched as our government became more and more Machiavellian. Politicians would say one thing during the campaign and then turn around and do the exact opposite once they got in office. I listened to Nancy Pelosi say things like, "If people are ripping your face off, you have to rip their face off." That sounds more like a capo on an FBI wiretap than the highest-ranking female elected official in US history. I read about guys like former House Majority Leader Tom DeLay, who once turned on a worker who had asked DeLay to douse his cigar because of federal smoke regulations. DeLay responded by shouting, "I *am* the federal government!" Bill Clinton lied about his affair with Monica Lewinsky while the guys trying to get him impeached—like Newt Gingrich—were having illicit affairs of their own.

It goes on and on. Lies, hypocrisy, entitlement. Politicians routinely act like the rules just don't apply to them. When I think of our elected leaders and the attitude they adopt in office, I think of the late Mob boss Carmine Galante. Galante, like DeLay, was often seen with a cigar in his mouth. "No one will ever kill me," he said once. "They wouldn't dare." Doesn't that make DeLay's elitist comment sound like an echo? Of course, Galante eventually was killed—gunned down in a restaurant assassination in 1979—and DeLay was forced to resign from Congress after being indicted and arrested for money laundering. He successfully appealed his conviction and then founded a lobbying firm. No surprise there!

The Mafia in America as well as in Italy has a long history in dealing with corrupt politicians. I personally dealt with some of them during my time in the life. But politicians behaving and governing like mobsters? That's another matter altogether, and that's definitely not good for America. You do not want the United States being governed by elected officials behaving like mobsters.

For a former made man like me, their behavior is evident. But I think the American public is not seeing our situation for what it is: a government being run by thugs. Our elected officials are supposed to represent our best interests, but instead they ruthlessly look out for themselves, solidifying their wealth and power and ignoring the people they were elected to support. John Wheeler III, an advisor to three Republican presidents, saw many of the same things I see. "Congress is a Mafia running a protection racket," Wheeler said.

This book will explore how US politicians have embraced

Machiavelli's ideology and exploited it the way a Mafia don would. Just as the Mafia extorted "protection money" from small businesses, the government overregulates businesses and stifles growth and healthy competition. Just as mobsters protect their profits and fund their businesses with "other people's money," politicians raid government coffers and run up massive debts that our children will be saddled with. Just as Cosa Nostra once controlled unions and reaped benefits from their pension funds, the government now supports unions by authorizing excessive compensation for unionized government workers, buying political support at the taxpayers' expense.

The result is a country where the wealthiest flourish while the average person falls behind, where soaring deficits threaten our economy, and where the public's disillusionment with elected officials and government has sent many to the streets to protest.

It's Time to Wake Up

This is not a book about my political views. This is not a partisan attempt to get people to go along with my politics or ideology. I'm not trying to get you to change political parties. I'm a conservative, but I'll spotlight the behavior of both Democrats and Republicans and show you how similar it is to how Mafia bosses act.

I want this book to serve as a wake-up call and help American citizens see what is really going on in the hallowed halls of Washington, DC. I want to alert people to the fact that our government is getting out of control and operating more like the Mafia than the representative government our founding fathers envisioned. And I want you to understand that it's dangerous. I know how the Mafia operates. I was born into it. I've lived it. It can be corrupt, vicious, and controlling. You don't want that in your government.

Our forefathers saw the danger of this and warned us about it. "Experience hath shewn, that even under the best forms, those entrusted with power have, in time and by slow operations, perverted it into tyranny," Thomas Jefferson wrote. "It is believed that the most effectual means of preventing this would be to illuminate, as far as practicable, the minds of the people at large."

I hope this book illuminates your mind and helps you see what's really happening. The idea that we are hiring altruistic, selfless, and honest representatives to protect our interests is outdated and naïve. Today's politicians are protecting their own interests, not ours, and we deserve better. This is not to say that *all* politicians are corrupt. From town halls to statehouses to Congress, honest people set aside their own interests to serve the people. We should respect and admire these folks. But whether you are a town selectman or freshman in Congress, it won't take long before you come face to face with blatant corruption veiled as "public service."

"Tyranny" the way Jefferson used it may sound like an exaggeration. Still, I think it's an apt description of what's happening in our government today. Look at the taxes we pay, the regulations we face. I've crisscrossed the country hundreds of times in recent years to give talks, and I hear the same things over and over. Small businesses can't turn a profit because of government red tape. Government services are slow, confusing, and uncompromising. People live in fear of the IRS, yet frauds like Bernie Madoff are openly stealing billions under the nose of federal regulators. How does this happen? Were the regulators grossly inept? Were they asleep at the wheel? Were they being paid off? Innocent people lost billions right under the nose of the federal regulators paid to protect them. Did any of them face consequences over this travesty? I think not. And why not? Obamacare has thrown a suffocating blanket over our healthcare, making most of us pay more for coverage so others can get cheaper insurance from government-run marketplaces. This is government meddling at its very worst, and it touches everyone's lives. Meanwhile, government subsidies and bailouts for industries that can afford to lobby Congress are sending our national deficit into the stratosphere.

People are tired, anxious, and uncertain. They need to know what is happening with their government, and that's what I aim to do with this book. To accomplish this goal, I'll explore the following:

- **The history of the Mafia in the US.** The Mob has a violent yet storied history in the United States. Though its influence has waned in recent years, its methods and ideology have flourished among elected officials across the country. I'll show you how the Mob was organized and how its structure and practices have been adopted by elected officials from your local statehouse to the halls of Congress.
- **The Invisible Empire of special interests that have captured our government.** President Woodrow Wilson warned us about this when he said, "The government, which was designed for the people, has got into the hands of the bosses and their employers, the special interests. An invisible empire has been set up above the forms of democracy." Wilson's grim observation seems even more prophetic today. Our elected leaders not only accept favors and contributions from lobbyists but work hand in glove with industries to develop policies that enrich corporations while leaving the rest of us struggling to make our house payments.

- **How politicians enrich themselves.** Again, John Murtha is not an outlier. He's the prototype for how politicians gain office and reap riches from their deals and corrupt allegiances. I'll explain how they manage this—and why there are more former Congressmen in prison today than there are Mafia bosses.
- **The role of lobbyists.** The Mafia's influence in places like New York, Chicago, Kansas City, and Las Vegas wasn't always based on the threat of violence. Instead, the Mob's power was often based on the promise of great wealth to those who did the Mafia's bidding. The same is true of lobbyists today. Lobbyists control government by allowing politicians to share in the wealth and security that comes from its tight grip on policy and regulations.
- **The price of overregulation.** The volume of federal regulations has tripled since 1970. Most of these rules don't affect industries with a strong lobbying arm, but the red tape pushes small businesses into bankruptcy and closes the door to innovators trying to enter a new market.
- **Campaign financing and term limits.** The vast sums of money required to win an election ensure that rich donors will get the ear of our elected leaders. But big money also encourages bigger government and drowns out the voices of regular citizens who want their representatives to address key social issues like abortion.

✵ Why I Wrote This Book ✵

In March of 2009, I was invited to be on the morning news show *Fox & Friends*, where I was supposed to talk about my new business book *I'll Make You an Offer You Can't Refuse*.

While I sat with Brian Kilmeade and Gretchen Carlson waiting to go on air, they asked some of the usual questions I get asked during first-time interviews. *How is it you quit the Mafia, refused government protection, and lived to tell about it? Where'd you hide all the money you made? Are you worried you'll get whacked?* Well, I replied, I didn't need government protection because I never testified against anyone in the Mafia. I didn't hide any money; it all went to the government for restitution. And no, I don't worry about getting whacked, but I also avoid routines and keep my eye out for suspicious characters.

Finally, the cameras lit up, and we were live in front of a few million people. Instead of asking me about my business book, Kilmeade asked me, "So Michael, is it a big stretch to suggest that Washington, DC, has become our 'Godfather'?"

It wasn't a question I expected, but I didn't hesitate to answer.

"I see a lot of similarities in the way they're operating and the way we used to operate on the street," I said.

I went on to talk about Timothy Geitner, the Treasury secretary at the time. Geitner was announcing the government's plan to battle The Great Recession, and I saw him as President Obama's "underboss" based on the way he was exercising control and doing the work of the whole family. We talked about Obama's consigliere (Joe Biden) and his caporegimes (Pelosi and Reid). I described billionaire philanthropist George Soros as "the guy in the shadows...pulling the strings on the (Democratic) party."

"I think this guy maintains a lot more control than we may think," I said. "He's got the money. He funds a lot of their groups. I really think he has a lot to say to that party."

"Michael, does it scare you?" Kilmeade asked.

"It concerns me," I replied. "Not much scares me at this point, but he (Soros) really concerns me."

That interview sowed the seeds for this book. Within minutes of leaving the studio, I was inundated with interview requests, and everyone wanted to talk about the Mafia Democracy I had described on *Fox & Friends*.

As I set out researching this book and putting some meat on the framework I'd sketched out on Fox, I became increasingly furious at what I saw happening in our government. It was even worse than I had imagined back in 2009. Again and again, I came across examples of government leaders deceiving Americans into believing politicians are servants of the people when, in fact, those elected representatives were getting fat on corrupt practices. I became convinced that we had a Mafia Democracy.

That's a pretty serious indictment of a democratic government that holds itself up to be the most honest, upright, and ethical governing body on the planet. That's what our founding fathers intended it to be. However, the architects of our constitution also warned their young country that their government *could* and most likely *would* be corrupted.

Again, Thomas Jefferson's words echo: "Experience hath shewn, that even under the best forms of government those entrusted with power have, in time, and by slow operations, perverted it into tyranny." Henry David Thoreau, the American historian and life-long abolitionist, issued a similar warning: "The government itself, which is only the mode which the people have chosen to execute their will, is equally liable to be abused and perverted before the people can act through it," he wrote in his essay *Civil Disobedience*. My friends, these are very serious statements from men who have both experienced and studied tyranny and corruption in the halls of a tyrannical government. These statements should sound the alarm, act as a wake-up call, and draw attention to what is happening in our government on both the federal and state, and even local levels.

In my opinion, our nation is in the throes of self-destruction as a result of morally bankrupt, self-serving politicians who place their own agendas above the needs of the people who elected them. The Mafia is just as good at making its members believe there is equality among them. But in reality, it exists to unequally benefit the people at the top at the expense of those it controls. I know. I lived the life.

And I believe that's what is happening in America. Many of our government leaders are deceiving Americans into believing they are servants of the people, and in the process, they are enriching themselves at the people's expense and to the people's detriment. I can recognize Mafia-like behavior when I see it, and I am seeing a pattern of such behavior among leaders of our government today.

America is not in the hands of patriots but rather in the grip of politicians who are gradually transforming America into a Mafia-style democracy. My hope is that the pages that follow will convince you that order needs to be restored in the beltway and in the offices of state and local governments nationwide. I honestly don't know if what is broken in government can be fixed or if history will repeat itself and America will see its demise from within its own borders as every other great power before it has.

I saw it happen with the crime families of New York when I was a Colombo family caporegime, and I'm seeing the same thing happen with our government. I'm sharing the similarities that I see between the Mafia and government with the hope that you won't be blindsided if our ever-expanding behemoth of a government ever collapses. If we don't do something, I believe that outcome is inevitable. "Remember," President John Adams once wrote, "Democracy never lasts long. It soon wastes, exhausts, and murders itself."

If we stand a chance to halt this steady dissolution of our

democracy, it will require that we all become aware of what's happening and start taking steps to stop it now, before it is too late.

Chapter I

The Rise and Fall of the Mafia

"It's better to spend one day as a lion, than one hundred years as a lamb."

—JOHN GOTTI

IN 1975, THE YEAR I BECAME A MADE MEMBER OF THE Colombo crime family in New York City, the Mafia influenced almost every corner of American society. We had political and economic power from New York, Boston, Philadelphia, Buffalo, Pittsburg, and Chicago to Las Vegas, Florida, and the West Coast. We infiltrated all the major unions, easily giving ourselves control over business leaders and politicians alike. We ran numbers. We fixed fights. We ran the construction industry and squeezed all the developers. We took a cut of every window installed in every skyscraper in Manhattan and every fish sold at the Fulton Fish Market. We controlled garbage collection. We controlled waterfront commerce in the nation's largest port. We laundered money. We loaned money. We had our hands in the record business. We collected a three-dollar "tax" on every article of clothing produced in Manhattan's garment district. We skimmed taxes meant for state governments and gaming control boards. We bribed cops, politicians, jurors, and judges. We extended credit to compulsive gamblers, and when they couldn't pay us back, we took over their businesses. We partnered with Jewish criminals, Russian mobsters, and Puerto Rican street gangs. For fun and front-pocket money, we owned car dealerships, nightclubs, and restaurants.

In 1975, the Mafia was a highly organized, hierarchical organization. Despite the occasional disagreement that led to bloodshed, the five families in New York City—the hub of organized crime worldwide—operated with grim efficiency. All major business initiatives, criminal activities, and assassinations had to be cleared by The Commission, the star chamber of family heads that tried to keep the peace, mediate disputes, and coordinate the vast array of criminal enterprises.

The families were run more like corporations than like street gangs. The bosses were the CEOs. The underbosses were the vice presidents. The caporegimes were the regional managers who ran the scams, organized the street crews, and collected the money. Our corporate structure allowed us to prosper, and our culture encouraged us to always be on the lookout for new ways to make money. We funded startups before anyone had ever heard of venture capitalists.

Machiavelli and the Mob

I mention all of this to help you understand the staggering scope and unrelenting ambition of the criminal operation I took a blood oath to serve. While most people associate the Mafia with violence, betrayal, deceit, and murder, it is also true that we were a shadowy, pervasive enterprise focused on expansion and profits. If we saw a way to make money, we did. If there was a way to improve the bottom line through extortion, bribery, or old-fashioned intimidation, we used it. We were like any profitable organization; we focused on growing profits, eliminating competition, and dodging taxes or any other constraints that might stand in our way of making money and manipulating markets.

We were so successful because we followed a cynical credo: We should appear to be merciful, humane, frank, and well-meaning, but when the need arose or when our power or authority was threatened, we must, as Machiavelli advised in *The Prince*, "be ready to take the way of evil." We understood that a wise guy should never keep a promise if circumstances changed and it was no longer in our best interest to honor that pledge. "The promise given was a necessity of the past," Machiavelli wrote in *The Prince*. "The word broken is a necessity of the present." And how often do politicians break their promises? How often do they raise taxes when they promised not to? How often do they assure us that their reasoning is sound and we find out later that there actually *weren't* any weapons of mass destruction or that the Taliban were, in fact, capable of seizing Afghanistan the second we evacuate? We've heard the lies and seen the deception all too many times.

Niccolò Machiavelli was born in the city-state of Florence in 1469 and became a senior official of diplomacy and military affairs in the Florentine Republic. He rose to prominence, though, as a Renaissance philosopher and writer. He wrote *The Prince* in 1513 to curry favor with the governor of Florence. Over the centuries, the book has been both dismissed by modern scholars as "evil recommendations to tyrants to help them maintain their power" and embraced by people like Dutch philosopher Baruch Spinoza as an "inspiration (for) modern democratic political philosophy." Bertrand Russell, the British philosopher who died in 1970, called it a book for gangsters.

Russell was correct. In the Mafia, *The Prince* was practically required reading. Why? It helped a made member to understand the ideology under which the Mafia operated. I read it in a prison cell near the end of my criminal career, and its messages resonated with me. Again and again, Machiavelli articulated principles that I'd grown up with and understood as if they were second nature. According to Machiavelli, the only way to maintain power is through ruthless cunning and deceit, and *Cosa Nostra* (Italian for "our thing") embraced this tenet in everything it did. Like Machiavelli, the Mob understood that in our neighborhoods, we needed to preserve the goodwill of the people. We needed to be generous and caring enough to gain the respect and loyalty of our communities because these people were our greatest asset. At the same time, we understood that threats and enemies to that community needed to be handled with brutal dispatch.

"People should either be caressed or crushed. If you do them minor damage, they will get their revenge; but if you cripple them, there is nothing they can do. If you need to injure someone, do it in such a way that you do not have to fear their vengeance." I can't read that quote without thinking about how the Democrats wrongly tried to use the impeachment process to not only get Donald Trump out of office but also to make it impossible for him to run for office again. Luckily, that effort failed.

Machiavelli also advised rulers to respect other men's property and women, and you see this reflected in the Mob's credo too. We respected other families' enterprises and territory. We came down hard on family members who cheated with other wise guys' wives or girlfriends. Mafia boss Salvatore Profaci said it best: "Goodfellas don't sue Goodfellas...Goodfellas kill Goodfellas."

When I was proposed for membership, I was twenty-one years old and on my way to becoming an experienced entrepreneur. I had a knack for launching and building successful businesses. I started shylocking when I was a teenager, and from there I moved on to opening body shops, used car lots, auto dealerships, and restaurants. The bosses were familiar with me because my father, John "Sonny" Franzese, had been a well-respected caporegime and one-time underboss of the Colombo family before being sent to prison. The Mob bosses had seen me grow up, picketing for Mafia boss Joe Colombo and his Italian-American Civil Rights League and playing shortstop for my Little League baseball team on Long Island. Although I'd been enrolled in Hofstra as a premed student, the bosses saw me as a "comer"—aggressive, motivated, and determined to succeed. When my dad proposed me for induction, I was a known entity and welcomed with open arms.

For me, the Mafia was like an accelerator. It widened the world and presented unimaginable opportunities to make money. Some guys in the Mob are what we might refer to as "workers" or "enforcers"—they settle scores, collect debts, and carry out orders at the behest of their superiors. And although every made man, myself included, had to prove themselves worthy by carrying out any order given to them as part of the family business, my skill was bringing in money, bags and bags stuffed with money. Within a few years of my being inducted, *Fortune* magazine reported that I had made more money for the Mob than anyone since Al Capone. Although I'd been getting hassled by cops and federal agents since I was an adolescent— thanks to my Dad's reputation with the Colombo family—being in the Mafia made me part of a powerful organization that stretched around the world. There was a lot of comfort and security in knowing that.

In those days, the Mob had a mythology about it. People romanticized it. Mario Puzo's novel *The Godfather* had come out in 1969, and *The Godfather* movies started coming out in 1972. Many of my colleagues were influenced by these portrayals of Mob families as equal parts warm-hearted integrity and cold-blooded ruthlessness. Sammy "The Bull" Gravano, for instance, saw *The Godfather* when he was in his late teens and said the film made him feel proud to be Italian and to join the Mafia. The public was similarly smitten, and many came to see the Mafia as some kind of modern-day version of Robin Hood and his band of merry men, stealing from the king and sharing the wealth with the common man. To many, we weren't murdering criminals. We just knew how to beat the system.

The Mafia in America

The Mafia got its start in Sicily, the big island at the toe of the boot-shaped shoreline of Italy. For centuries, Sicily was ruled by foreign invaders, so islanders formed their own bands of men to keep the order and maintain some kind of control over local affairs. There was nothing criminal about their work; mafioso, or Mafia members, were suspicious of central authorities and tried to protect their women, children, and villages from exploitation at the hands of the Arabs, French, Spanish, and Romans who occupied their lands. According to *Five Families: The Rise, Decline, and Resurgence of America's Most Powerful Mafia Empires,* the term Mafia is a Sicilian-Arabic slang expression for someone "acting as a protector against the arrogance of the powerful."

They had their own code of conduct, known as *omerta*, which held that people should never go to their government for justice and never cooperate with government agents investigating wrongdoing. Justice would be served by the Mafia. These scattered Mafia clans also adopted secret rituals and induction ceremonies in which newly proposed members pledged utter loyalty to their new family.

The Mafia's authority deepened and spread; even officials in Rome sought help from the Mafia to control independent bands of criminals that terrorized the rocky Sicilian landscape. Although the Romans saw this as a stopgap measure that would fade as the new country solidified its power, the Mafia used the arrangement to expand their hold on the island. They extorted crop protection from absentee landlords, shook down merchants in the larger towns, and hampered the work of tax collectors from Rome.

The Mafia continued to exert control in Sicily after the island became an Italian province in the mid-1800s. Mafia families expanded their influence, forcing landowners to pay for protection, bribing politicians, and intimidating voters during elections. And, in the same way *The Godfather* and *Goodfellas* movies popularized the gangster life, an 1860s play called *I Mafiusi de la Vicaria* (Heroes of the Penitentiary) toured Italy and glamorized the customs and traditions of the small armies (*mafie*) that ruled the Sicilian countryside.

Starting in 1890, rural Sicilians who were tired of the lawlessness of their homeland began migrating to the United States. Mafia clans went with them, establishing first in New Orleans, where they quickly took over the city's stevedore operations, and later flooding into New York City. By 1920, more than four million Italians from Sicily and southern Italy were crowded into the New York neighborhoods of Little Italy, East Harlem, and

Williamsburg. Irish gangs owned the West Side of Manhattan while the Jews owned the Lower East Side. In these years, the Mafia focused primarily on the Italian neighborhoods.

In time, however, two significant events would reshape the Mafia in America. The first was Mussolini's rise to power and the Fascist movement in Italy, and the second was Prohibition in America. The first drove even more Italian criminals to the US, and the second gave them a steady source of revenue to vastly expand their criminal enterprise in their new country.

Mussolini and the Mafia

Benito Mussolini rose to power in Italy in the 1920s. He gained prominence as the editor of a socialist newspaper opposed to Italy entering World War I but then quickly changed his position. He left the Socialist party and, backed by France and Italian industrialists, advocated for war against Austria.

Mussolini's inconsistency reflected the general political and economic chaos in Italy, and when he returned from fighting, Mussolini pushed for the country to find a leader "ruthless and energetic enough to make a clean sweep." After being elected Italy's youngest prime minister, Mussolini managed to do this, steadily dismantling Italy's democratic institutions while solidifying his power. At rallies jammed with his black-shirted followers, he used his imposing physical stature and thunderous, pounding rhetoric to propel himself to the dictatorship of his Fascist regime.

As a northerner from the Venetian Alps north of Udine, Mussolini had it in for the Mafia clans that operated in Sicily and the south. He saw the Mafia as a threat to his power, and he also hated them for personal reasons. As compared to his packed rallies in the northern parts of Italy, during a 1924 visit to

Sicily, the only people who turned out for Mussolini's speech in the central plaza was a group of homeless beggars and mentally handicapped residents rounded up by the mayor. At another speech in Sicily, someone stole Mussolini's hat.

Machiavellian in his own right, Mussolini set out to crush the Mafia. More than a thousand Mafia members were thrown in jail or tortured in the late 1920s, leading to a diaspora of the Sicilian Mob to America. Although unfettered entry to the US was slowed by immigration laws, Sicilian gangsters still found their way to America through Cuba and other access points.

Prohibition

As Italians flooded into New York, a business opportunity presented itself: the Eighteenth Amendment to the Constitution, which made the production and sale of alcoholic beverages a federal crime. Ironically, Prohibition was in part inspired by the United States' concern about the growing decadence of big cities being flooded with immigrants. But Prohibition didn't curtail that corruption; it accelerated it. People like Joseph Bonanno, who arrived in New York at the age of nineteen, built stills and quickly began raking in huge profits from liquor sales. "I thought (bootlegging) was too good to be true," Bonanno wrote sixty years later. "I didn't consider it wrong. It seemed fairly safe in that the police didn't bother you. There was plenty of business for everyone."

The stills soon gave way to more sophisticated breweries and smuggling operations to bring in Canadian and British whisky. The industry also slid into violence as the Jewish and Irish gangs battled the Italians for territory and control of some other emerging criminal enterprises, such as gambling. The largest Italian family at the time, led by Giuseppe "Joe" Masseria, killed dozens of rivals and refused to make peace with any rival. The bloodshed threatened to topple the bootlegging industry until a young lieutenant in the Masseria family, Lucky Luciano, brokered alliances with such prominent Jewish gangsters as Meyer Lansky and Benjamin "Bugsy" Siegel. Luciano arranged to have Joe Masseria killed, ushering in a new generation of English-speaking mobsters who discredited the hidebound, outdated practices of Old Word "Mustache Pete" mobsters like Masseria.

The Golden Years

Prohibition helped the families get a firm foothold in the Northeast, and our code of honor and secrecy was what Joe Bonanno called "the glue that held us together." Bonanno and Luciano worked together to bring the five dominant families together on what Joe called the "path of peace." They formalized the Mafia power structure: each family had a boss as well as a sottocapo, or underboss, and a consigliere, an advisor who settled intrafamily differences and negotiated quiet agreements with other families. Only men whose parents came from Sicily or southern Italy were granted membership, and the size of families were fixed, with new blood coming in only when a made guy died. Membership was for life. You didn't get to retire or change professions. "The purpose of the code," said *New York Times* organized crime expert Selwyn Raab, "was to withstand any assault by law enforcement…and to enable the family to continue functioning efficiently, even if the boss or other hierarchs were removed."

Luciano introduced the idea of what came to be known as "The Commission," the Mob bosses who dictated the regulations for all organized crime operations. The bosses came from the five New York families, as well as members from Buffalo and Chicago. The central goal was to prevent violence and to finally cut all ties to the Old World gangs still operating in Sicily. Luciano did not want the American families to be subsidiaries of the Sicilian Mafia; he wanted the new families to be independent and free to adapt to the new political and cultural characteristics of the US. The New Yorkers called themselves *Cosa Nostra* instead of the Mafia, while Al Capone's crew in Chicago went by "the Outfit" and Buffalo's Stefano Magaddino called his gang "the Arm."

Prohibition ceased in 1933 with the adoption of the Twenty-first Amendment. This ended the Mafia's monopoly over alcohol, but they soon found a new way to control the economy of New York and elsewhere: unions. Mob guys moved in quickly. Some ran for and won offices within the unions, and others cozied up to existing union bosses and got them working for the Mafia through intimidation, bribes, extortion, or outright partnerships. In turn, the Mob showed the union guys how to enrich themselves without getting caught by the feds or by the union membership.

The Mafia infiltrated the Teamsters Union, the Tailor and Cutters Union, the Fur and Leather Workers Union, the Longshoremen's Union, hotel and restaurant workers, the United Brotherhood of Carpenters and Joiners, and the Laborers International Union of North America. At one point, the Mob controlled about twenty locals and a few international unions. For decades, it handpicked union presidents, put Mob guys on high-paying union salaries, and skimmed and "borrowed" millions to fund outside projects. What's more, as union "reps," Mob guys could now meet openly with politicians and business leaders; while a Mob boss wouldn't get through the door, a union executive, even one with ties to the Mafia, had no trouble gaining access and greasing palms with campaign contributions, bribes, and thinly veiled threats of labor strikes and election fraud. The Mafia could promise union support to candidates who tacitly agreed to never investigate or indict them.

Union Benefits

When you controlled a union, there was no end to how you could make money. We squeezed employers by threatening strikes that would shut them down. If they didn't pay, we'd order the union to stop work and to start picketing, or else we'd move into work sites and sabotage equipment or property. Employers paid us so we would let them ignore the costly terms of their collective bargaining agreements (that's where the term "sweetheart deal" comes from), and many paid us just to keep the peace on a job site. In some industries, we forced businesses to form cartels, which allowed members to control prices and gave us a steady income from dues. Anyone who tried to go around the cartel and hire someone else ran the risk of getting shut down, and heaven help any company that tried to buck the cartel.

If your business involved shipping, construction, manufacturing, or entertainment, you worked with us. Your contractors were our contractors. Your imports and exports were loaded and unloaded by us. The meals you made at your restaurant were served by us. We had a million ways to make your life miserable if you refused our terms. If you were a longshoreman, you had to pay kickbacks to the union boss to get work. If you were a shipper, you had to pay extra to get your cargo unloaded. We made money from both sides at once, stealing funds from the unions' welfare and pension funds and extorting employers who didn't play our game. For instance, if you ran a parking garage and didn't hire union workers, our guys made it a point to slash your customers' tires, tear up their fine upholstery, and scratch up their paint jobs until you did.

The beauty was that both sides of the labor movement invited us in. By the time Prohibition ended, labor wars in the US had been going on for decades. Workers got the shit kicked out of them by employers, and employers were tired of labor violence and the growing menace of communists and leftists who were finding followers in the union ranks. Both sides asked for our help. According to Howard Kimeldorf, who wrote the book *Reds or Rackets?*, in 1988, the Mob was less threatening to businessmen, government officials, and union leaders than communist activists.

We were happy to oblige.

The government started holding hearings about the Mob's involvement in labor in the 1950s. At the time, you'd have gotten the impression from the newspapers that the Mob controlled every Italian in New York City. This was not the case, but you could understand why people would think otherwise.

Actor and screenwriter Chazz Palminteri grew up in the Bronx in the 1950s and saw the Mafia firsthand. He witnessed a Mob murder when he was nine years old, but when police came to question him, Palminteri insisted he hadn't seen anything. He would go on to write *A Bronx Tale*—a one-man play that tells the story of a young Italian boy from a working-class family who gets drawn into Mob life. From Palmenteri's perspective, though, Cosa Nostra was just one aspect of the Italian community at the time.

"I'm very proud of being Italian-American, but people don't realize that the Mafia is just this aberration," said Palminteri, who went on to star in the movie version of his play. "The real community is built on the working man, the guy who's the cop, the fireman, the truck driver, the bus driver." Very wise words written by the man I have come to know, love, and respect.

The Mob still had a firm grip on the labor rackets when I was proposed in 1972. A few years later, in 1975, Teamsters president Jimmy Hoffa disappeared. Hoffa had been convicted of pension fund fraud and jury tampering in 1964 but was pardoned by Nixon in 1971. When he got out of prison, Hoffa tried to wrest control of the Teamsters from his stand-in, Frank Fitzsimmons, but the families liked Fitzsimmons and didn't trust Hoffa. As a result, Jimmy Hoffa disappeared. His disappearance in 1975 has been the subject of countless books, movies, media reports, and speculation. Some of us did not speculate, however. Some of us knew, for a fact, that Hoffa was murdered. And yes, it was a Mob-contracted hit. But Jimmy Hoffa is not the subject of this book.

Even when this was all blowing up, we continued to benefit from the union rackets for years. In 1983, a Department of Labor investigation found that in Chicago alone, eighty-five labor organizations were affiliated with parent unions with ties to the Mob. Jackie Presser, the president of the International Brotherhood of Teamsters, was the son of Chicago Mob boss Bill Presser, who managed the Teamsters Central States Pension Fund. While most pension funds at the time invested less than 10 percent of their money into real estate, Bill Presser funneled 70 percent of his son's Teamster's fund into Mob-sponsored real estate ventures, including high-rise casinos in Las Vegas.

It's hard to overstate the political leverage unions gave us. While senators, with their long terms and statewide constituency, were somewhat immune to our pressure, members of the House of Representatives were not. They faced reelection every two years, and few could afford to offend their local unions or turn down union campaign money. When Rudy Giuliani, then the US Attorney for the Southern District of New York, prepared a civil racketeering case against the Teamsters in 1986, Jackie Presser showed just how much political clout the union hefted; using a well-funded lobbying and public relations campaign, Presser persuaded two hundred senators and representatives in Congress to sign a Justice Department petition against the suit.

Giuliani filed it anyway in 1988, and less than a year later, the Teamsters and government agreed to a consent decree that purged most Mafia figures from the union and set up a panel to oversee other union reforms. For the next several years, the Justice Department went after one mobbed-up union after another.

Giuliani and RICO

Although the Racketeer Influenced and Corrupt Organizations (RICO) Act was enacted in 1970, it took ten years before prosecutors, led by Giuliani, figured out how to best use it against us. The government first used RICO in 1979 to go after Anthony Scotto, (passed away in August of 2021) of the Gambino family, who controlled the International Longshoremen's Association. I was very familiar with Scotto. He did prison time with my father, and I had several conversations with him about union business in the visiting room. RICO made it a serious federal offense to participate in organized crime activity, and all a prosecutor had to show was a "pattern of behavior" rather than a specific crime. This made it significantly easier for prosecutors to win a case in court. Under RICO, a Mob boss could be convicted of merely *ordering* a hit, and the penalties were almost as bad and oftentimes worse than if he'd killed the guy himself.

RICO allowed prosecutors to freeze our assets, preventing us from hiding our money, and it carried long prison sentences and staggering financial penalties. RICO made it much tougher to launder money through legitimate businesses, and it allowed civil claims that increased the financial penalties. Suddenly, guys like me who could easily win our criminal cases—I beat four state cases and one federal racketeering case in ten years—were looking at long prison sentences and huge fines.

Giuliani dealt the Mafia a crippling blow when he indicted eleven made men, including several of the bosses in The Commission trial in 1985, on charges of extortion, racketeering, and murder for hire. My boss, Carmine Persico, got swept up in that case and was sentenced to a hundred years in prison. Tony Salerno of the Genovese family received the same sentence, as did the other bosses. The case essentially wiped out the Mafia's central committee in New York City and broke up our control of the concrete industry in the city and the garbage-hauling business on Long Island. *Time* magazine called it the "Case of Cases" and "the most significant assault on the infrastructure of organized crime" in forty years.

Ironically, it was a boneheaded move by one of our bosses, Joe Bonanno, that paved the way for Giuliani's RICO cases against the Mob. Bonanno had written his autobiography, *A Man of Honor,* and in it he mapped out the entire organizational structure of the five families, along with the succession lines going back to the 1930s. Bonanno thought he was being crafty because the statute of limitations had expired on all of the crimes he described in the book. But Bonanno apparently hadn't read the RICO statute. RICO crimes had no statute of limitations, and Bonanno's book gave Giuliani everything he needed to start building his case against The Commission. "Bonanno just laid the whole thing out for us," Giuliani told me in a YouTube sitdown I had with him years later. "He gave us half our case in that book."

The Mob already knew Bonanno was a liability. In fact, he'd been put on a hit list. But instead of killing him, the Mob sent him packing to Arizona with instructions to keep a low profile and to quit bothering the families. He didn't listen and instead did the worst thing he could possibly do by writing a tell-all book that gave Giuliani the heavy-gauge ammunition he needed.

The Commission case altered the Mob forever. Our leadership was gone, and the whole notion of *omerta*—our code of secrecy and honor—was dealt a fatal blow. The feds had wiretaps everywhere—the one they planted in the dashboard of Mob soldier Salvatore Avellino's Jaguar gave them all the information they needed to build their case against The Commission. And, facing sentences of fifty to a hundred years in prison, one guy after another rolled over and decided to testify.

This is the atmosphere I was operating in when I was indicted in December 1985 on fourteen counts of racketeering, counterfeiting, and extortion. A 1986 cover story in *Fortune* named me as number eighteen on *Fortune* magazine's list of the "Fifty Most Wealthy and Powerful Mafia Bosses." I had a helicopter, multiple homes, and a private plane to travel between them.

For the last seven years, we'd been running a gasoline bootlegging scheme in which we'd sell gas to stations at below-market prices and pocket the state, local, and federal taxes. We worked through phony Panama companies, and when government agents would start asking questions, we'd close the dummy company and open a new one. We set up a sheaf of eighteen companies and obtained wholesale licenses from shady politicians I was paying off to obtain them. At the height of the operation, we were making about $8 million a week. At the same time, I owned car dealerships, leasing companies, auto repair shops, restaurants, nightclubs, a contractor company, video stores, travel agencies, and a movie production and distribution company.

Although I had beat a racketeering charge in April of 1985, later that year I was indicted again, first in Florida and then in New York. The Florida RICO indictment included 177 counts and twenty-six codefendants. Those charges focused on my gasoline business. The New York racketeering indictment included twenty-eight counts that had been put together by a fourteen-agency task force. Only one count focused on the gasoline business; the rest accused me of conspiracy, mail fraud, obstruction of justice, extortion, embezzlement, and wire fraud. The last count was a "Kline conspiracy" that claimed every business I owned—twenty-one in all—was created for the sole purpose of stealing taxes. Although I do admit to being guilty of some of the charges, the government certainly embellished many.

Not long ago, I appeared with Giuliani on a podcast hosted by Joe Pagliarulo (*The Joe Pags Show*, iHeart radio). Believe it or not, it was good to see the old prosecutor again. I hadn't seen him in nearly thirty-eight years—since the day during my trial when he'd shown up to confer with the prosecutors from his office who were handling my case. My father had previously gone to prison on a fifty-year sentence, and I remember Rudy giving my attorney, John Jacobs, a word of warning: "Your client can get double what his father got," I heard Giuliani say. "A hundred years." I remember how Giuliani's clipped, terse assertion left a cold pit in my stomach.

The Plea Deal

I didn't think the case against me was that strong, but as I sat in my cell in the Metropolitan Correctional Center in New York, one mobster after another was losing in court and getting heavy, heavy sentences. Thirty years. Fifty years. One hundred years. To make matters worse, my friend and former partner in the gasoline business, Larry Iorizzo, had become a government informant. He had testified in my last trial and would be a key witness on these new charges. The government also seemed to have targeted me specifically. Although my crimes were essentially white-collar offenses, I was denied bail while the "Dapper Don" himself, John Gotti, and his associates walked free on bond. I also knew that federal prosecutors were already working up a detailed indictment on the gasoline tax scam. Those charges would be much tougher to beat.

And, in truth, I was not the same fearless capo who had already won five trials. I'd met my new wife Cammy the year before, and we had a newborn baby. Cammy had introduced me to what would be a life-transforming experience in accepting the Christian faith. She loved me, but she was terrified of the world I came from. In her mind, we had more to fear from our friends than we did from prosecutors. In my most recent trial, one of my codefendants, Vincent Rotondo, was gunned down while seated in his car in front of his home in Mill Basin, allegedly because one of his associates had turned informant. He'd gone out to get some fish for dinner and was shot in front of his home while his wife and kids waited inside.

Cammy was not cut out for this kind of business. She had not grown up with it the way I had. And although her father was a bit of a neighborhood rabble-rouser, Cammy was a devout Christian, raised by a mother who was a godly woman. The one and only experience she had with the Mafia was in watching *The Godfather*.

So, instead of fighting the charges against me, I instructed my lawyer to negotiate a plea with the Justice Department. The feds were hungry for a conviction. Having won five trials and beating Giuliani in my last RICO trial gave my attorney the leverage he needed to negotiate a good deal. I pled guilty to two of the twenty-six federal charges and to sixty-five of the Florida charges. I was sentenced to nine years in the state case to run concurrently with a ten-year prison sentence I was given in the federal case. I forfeited $5 million in assets and was ordered to pay $10 million in fines and restitution. The terms of my plea agreement did not require me to cooperate with the government, provide information, or testify against my former associates. In private, I admitted that I planned to leave the Mafia. In return for the guilty plea, prosecutors agreed to clear me of any past unknown crimes that might have been committed up until the day I took the plea—with the exception of murder or perjury.

Gaining Freedom

When I was finally released from parole in 1995, Cosa Nostra was a shadow of its former self. The big families in New York and Chicago still had some operations going on, but most of the old Mob bosses were dead or in prison. Gotti, the "Teflon Don" considered by many to be the face of the Mafia in New York, had died of throat cancer in prison in 1992. The head of the Lucchese family, Alphonse D'Arco, had turned informant and brought down more than fifty guys. The five families had about six thousand members and associates when I went into prison, but when I got out, the FBI estimated there were only half that number, and they were scattered all over the country. You could still find them in New York, Florida, Philly, Boston, Providence, Buffalo, and a few other big cities, but they weren't wielding the power and influence they had during my time in the life.

Even the streets were not the same. Our old hangouts were gone, and the smart, young Italians—guys like me who knew how to start businesses, form allegiances, and get things done—were not interested in the Mob life. They wanted to launch tech startups or get jobs where the real money was being made—on Wall Street, where it was still legal to cheat people out of their money. "The families no longer attract young men with brains," former New York detective Ralph Salerno told *The New York Times* reporter Selwyn Raab. "Now they want to be CEOs of legitimate corporations."

When Frank Cali, the head of the Gambinos, was shot down in 2019, it was among the first high-profile Mob hits since the early-nineties Persico-Orena war, when Vittorio "Little Vic" Orena challenged Carmine Persico for control of the Colombo crime family. That war left more than ten mobsters dead. The Cali hit nearly thirty years later prompted a lot of people to suggest that the Mob was back to its old tricks. But the truth is that the killer, a twenty-four-year-old who lived with his parents, was mentally unstable and shot Cali because he thought the mobster was part of the "deep state" working to discredit Donald Trump.

The New Mob

Today, although I took a blood oath in 1975, I no longer consider myself a made man, and I have no further involvement in Cosa Nostra. I formally walked away around the time my parole ended in 1996. I know this angered my old boss, Carmine Persico, and that it's very likely that he ordered a hit on me. But in my new life with Cammy in California, I was careful not to make mistakes that would give my former associates an opportunity to retaliate against me for walking away. I kept the bills out of my name. I didn't eat at the same place every day. I walked my dog in different neighborhoods. I did not live in fear, and I was prepared to retaliate if I had to. But since I had moved away, never testified against any former associates, and never put anyone in jail, my former Mob associates have moved on from me. Don't get me wrong; Mob guys are very proficient in carrying out the Mob's business, and I never sell them short. But I am certainly not a priority. They have concerns far more important than myself. Carmine Persico, my former boss and possibly the only Mob guy who might still have had a grudge against me, died in prison in 2019 at the age of eighty-five while serving a 139-year sentence. To me, his death, along with the death of my father in 2020, felt like my final binding tie to the Mafia had been broken.

Yet, a nagging sense that I was still in that life seemed to persist. I didn't understand it at first. I couldn't put a finger on what was haunting me.

Around 2004, just seven years after my parole ended, Cammy and I took a vacation to Maui. I had started to follow politics. Although I'm a Republican, I had watched the Democratic National Convention on TV that summer and had caught a speech given by a young state senator from Illinois named Barack Obama. His speech had filled me full of hope for the political future of our country. Obama talked about his father, who grew up herding goats in Kenya. He talked about how the government couldn't solve all of our problems, but it could make sure it gave all our children a "decent shot at life." He talked about the importance of community, faith, and service.

He spoke to me.

As Cammy and I walked along the beach in Maui that day, I glanced up and saw a slender Black man on the beach with his wife.

"That's the guy from the convention," I said to Cammy. "Obama."

"Barack Obama," she said.

"Right. Hell of a speech."

As it happened, our paths on that beach merged, and when we were close to the young politician and his wife, Michelle, I greeted him and complimented him on his speech. Is it true, I asked, that you might someday run for president?

"We're thinking about it," Obama said with that loose, confident grin.

As I watched Obama win the presidency four years later and begin to push his agenda, though, the optimism and enthusiasm I'd felt on that beach evaporated. He espoused lofty principles but governed with a cold disregard for personal freedom. He spied on his own people. He battled the media's efforts to unseal secrets. On the campaign trail, he decried lobbyists and corrupt campaign finance laws, but while in office, he embraced cronyism and gave free access to the rich contributors who gave to his campaign. His senior advisors and Cabinet officials faced charges of tax impropriety, conflicts of interest, and other ethical infractions. Obama, it became clear to me, wanted to insert government control over our lives. He wanted power over us, and he'd turned to a parade of corrupt politicians to achieve it. From The Great Recession bailout to the Affordable Care Act, the Dodd–Frank bill, and his response to the Arab Spring, Obama's agenda was to weaken our country and redistribute its wealth.

He was not the man who gave the speech at the Democratic National Convention in July 2004. He was not the same politician we had elected.

For me, a light snapped on.

Obama had promised us one thing and given us something different. Obama gave hope to some and cruelly crushed others.

Just like a mobster. Machiavellian.

The promise given was a necessity of the past, Machiavelli said. *The word broken is a necessity of the present.*

A wise Prince cannot and should not keep his pledge when it is against his interest to do so and when his reasons for making the pledge are no longer operative.

And so was born the premise for this book. The Mafia had its way in this country for seventy-five years before people like Rudy Giuliani blew the whistle and found a way to stop them. But while our lawmen were focused on bringing down one evil, a new one—our government—was forming.

And it was based on the same principles as the Mafia.

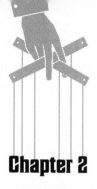

Chapter 2

The Invisible Empire

"The downfall of every civilization comes, not from the moral corruption of the common man, but rather from the moral complacency of common men in high places."

—E. DIGBY BALTZELL

IN 2007, CONGRESS PASSED A NEW ETHICS LAW THAT WAS supposed to put an end to elected leaders accepting many of the campaign contributions, gifts, favors, loans, and perks that they'd been receiving for decades from special interests.

The new law was considered the most thorough ethics reform measure since Watergate. It came on the heels of scandals involving Jack Abramoff, the lobbyist who'd gone to jail the year before for giving illegal gifts and making campaign contributions in return for votes and support from politicians like Bob Ney and Tom DeLay.

Almost immediately, federal lawmakers began looking for ways around the new rules. Like a mobster forbidden by his bosses to sell drugs will find ways to do so to make a buck. For example, a month after the new law passed, about one hundred members of Congress attended black-tie galas as guests of corporations and lobbyists, who paid as much as $2,500 for each ticket. It would have been illegal for the lobbyists to actually *hand over* the expensive tickets, so they just left them at a will-call window for the politicians to pick up.

Hell, the politicians wrote the law. They should know how to sidestep it. You can bet that as they were writing the law, the writers already knew how to circumvent it. So much of what corrupt politicians do is to put on a show for the people.

Fun, free evenings in tuxes was just one example of how our elected leaders ignored the law they wrote to prevent their ethical conflicts. The new law also put an end to the politicians' practice of booking several commercial flights and canceling the less convenient ones without paying a cancellation fee. This was special treatment, and the airlines were glad the new law would put an end to it.

Or did it? Less than a month after the new ethics law was approved, Senate leaders Harry Reid and Mitch McConnell—in a quaint, heartwarming gesture of bipartisan teamwork—slipped some language into a defense appropriations bill that allowed elected officials to continue booking as many seats as they wanted. "Welcome to the world of skirting around the rules we pass," one Senate staffer wrote to a lobbyist at the time.

It's almost as if our elected "leaders" are tearing a page out of *The Prince*, where Machiavelli tells rulers that it's okay to be two-faced if it helps retain their power. Leaders need to *appear* to be honorable (by passing laws defining what they consider to be ethical behavior), but they don't have to *behave* honorably (by actually following those rules). That's why Reid and McConnell publicly offered full-throated support for new rules but privately found ways around them.

My Own Experience

When I was a young man getting established in business on Long Island, I didn't hold politicians in high regard. After years of watching my father deal with law enforcement and federal agents, I had a low opinion of the government and politicians in general.

But after I was initiated into the Mob, my capo taught me how to use politicians for the work we were doing. Mobsters often have a reputation for being rough and threatening, but some of us were well-dressed and polished. We were respectful and polite. You needed to be this way if you wanted favors from a politician.

Both my captain and Genovese Mob capo, Fred "Fritzy" Giovanelli, also a dear friend, were close to Meade Esposito, the Democratic leader from Brooklyn, and we attended fundraisers together. I learned how to handle politicians and how it might be useful to get to know them better. A lot of politicians ate at one of our restaurants, Crisci's, in the Greenpoint section of Brooklyn. On any given day, you could find judges sitting at one table, prosecutors at another table, politicians sitting at a different table, and mobsters mingling among them.

The secret with politicians was to get them to trust you. You aren't trying to strike fear into their hearts. Instead, you want them to understand that there's an advantage in working with you. If you were well known, if you were taking care of your neighborhood and keeping people happy, if you were well mannered and discreet, the politicians would gravitate to you. You took care of things for them. You bribed them, of course, but you also got them a new car when they needed it, or helped them with their events and fundraisers. You became indispensable to them, so when you needed a favor, they obliged.

The same thing is going on today, although mobsters like

me have been replaced by legitimate businesses. Consider these cases:

- William Jefferson, a Democrat from Louisiana, served in the House of Representatives for nine terms until 2009, when he was sentenced to thirteen years in prison. He was accused of collecting a $500,000 bribe from an IT company in return for touting the company's products to the military. When the FBI raided his office, they found stacks of bills wrapped in aluminum foil and stuffed into a pie-crust box in the Congressman's freezer.
- Nancy Nord, the chief of the Consumer Product Safety Commission, took dozens of trips paid for by the toy, appliance, and children's furniture industries she was regulating. She and her predecessor took trips to China, Spain, San Francisco, New Orleans, and Hilton Head Island, where they stayed at a golf resort. They called it research.
- Randy Cunningham, a Republican representative from California, got eight years in prison in 2005 after taking $2.4 million in bribes from defense contractors. "Duke," as he was called, had served honorably in the US Navy as a fighter pilot for twenty years before going to Washington and landing a seat on the Defense Appropriations Subcommittee. He sold his $900,000 home in Del Mar, California to a defense contractor for twice what it was worth, and when he was in Washington, he lived on a yacht owned by the same guy. Meanwhile, the defense contractor got tens of millions of dollars in defense contracts.

I could go on, and I will in later chapters. But suffice it to say for now that it's not hard to find stories about elected officials—or regulators like Nancy Nord—who receive unethical rewards from special interests. These rewards are not always considered bribes, but the effect is the same: our elected leaders benefit from the people they are supposed to keep at arm's length.

And it's getting worse.

The Flow of Lobbyist Money

From 1998 to 2019, lobbyists reported spending $3.5 billion to influence public policy. The number is probably only half of what they actually spent. And again, let's be clear here. It's called "lobbying" when it's done in Congress, but anywhere else it is known as a "bribe," pure and simple. I wasn't "lobbying" when I was funneling cash to lawmakers in Albany for wholesale licenses that enabled my eighteen Panamanian companies to collect the gasoline taxes on behalf of the government. By whatever name, the effect is the same: you are paying to influence politicians and to get what you want.

Take the pharmaceutical industry for example. During the COVID pandemic of 2020 and 2021, some of these companies received billions of dollars from the federal government to develop vaccines, boosting their stock prices and making some executives instant billionaires. The government's decision to dole out billions to these firms came at the same time that drug companies were spending record amounts on lobbying. According to the website Open Secrets, Big Pharma spent $92 million on lobbying in the first three months of 2021 alone. The Pharmaceutical Research and Manufacturers of America, the nation's largest pharmaceutical trade association and typically the industry's biggest lobbying investor, led the way by spending $8.7 million to influence Congress, and Pfizer spent $3.7 million. During that time, Pfizer reported making $3.5 billion in profits from sales of the vaccine during the first three months of 2021.

COVID profiteering aside, since 2000, the amount of money corporations and others spend on lobbying has doubled. Lobbyists spend more than the entire operating budget of the House and the Senate combined. The biggest spenders include the pharmaceuticals and health products industry, which spent $300 million—nearly twice the next highest-spending industry. (Ever wonder why the cost of prescriptions and medications are so high?) Insurance companies and electronics manufacturers spent $150 million each, followed by oil and gas companies, business associations, hospitals, and electric utilities. Again, who suffers and who benefits from Mob-like behavior?

According to Lee Drutman, a senior fellow at the political reform program at New America, some of the biggest companies have as many as one hundred lobbyists, allowing them "to be everywhere, all the time." Of the top hundred organizations that lobby, ninety-five represent business. The rest are a smattering of labor unions and public interest groups.

And lobbying is just a part of what large corporations spend on trying to influence the government. It doesn't count the campaign contributions these same groups make or the research and strategizing they conduct to support their legislative positions. Lobbyists do everything they can to insert themselves into government actions, just like Mob guys bribing officials with bricks of laundered cash.

What this means is that big business is stealing our lawmakers' attention. They are ignoring you and me. I don't know about you, but I can't afford to open an office on K Street in DC so I can get a meeting with someone in Congress. I'm not leaving $2,500 tickets at will-call for my representative. I can't afford to send my senator to Hilton Head for a few rounds of golf.

And I'm not alone. According to the Gallup Poll, one of the highest priorities of most Americans for almost ten years now has been "reducing corruption in the federal government." Almost 90 percent of us find that important or extremely important. The only thing Americans care more about is creating good jobs.

It's not just Congress either. This same kind of influence peddling is going on in statehouses around the country. According to University of California political scientist Charlotte Hill, forty-nine out of fifty states have more registered lobbying entities than they do actual elected officials. In my state, California, there are thirty lobbying groups for every lawmaker. Did you read that? THIRTY lobbying groups for every lawmaker. They are all there for one reason: to bribe public officials for favors for their clients. It's no surprise that California is one of the most regulated states in the nation. Nationwide, lobbying groups outnumber state legislators by a six-to-one margin.

And it's all about business. Almost 85 percent of the fifty largest lobbying groups operating in state capitals represent business interests.

Lobbying and the First Amendment

Lobbyists were not always so closely associated with corruption and bribery. The first lobbyist was a former Revolutionary War officer named William Hull. In 1792, he traveled to Philadelphia—the new nation's first capital—to press elected leaders to give soldiers back pay. Hull wrote letters, chatted with President Washington, and recruited veterans' groups to help.

Hull lost, but his effort was nevertheless considered a constitutional right protected by the First Amendment. In those days, many founding fathers were still alive and happy to point out that citizens of the United States had every right to "petition the Government for a redress of grievances." Petition as a citizen, not bribe like a mobster.

James Madison, for instance, wrote in Federalist No. 10 that he didn't consider "special interests" to be "an evil to be eradicated." He thought factions were "sown in the nature of man" and that the role of government was to find a way to "regulate competing interests by involving the spirit of those interests in the ordinary operations of government." In other words, lobbying was central to the work of making policy.

Hull might be a good example of how lobbying was supposed to work, but his approach was soon corrupted by others who wanted to influence elected officials. By the 1850s, arms maker Samuel Colt was handing out free pistols in Washington in an effort to convince politicians to extend his patent on revolvers. In 1875, lobbyist Sam Ward was accused of passing out $100,000 in bribes to politicians.

By the early 1900s, President Woodrow Wilson started railing about "an invisible empire" of lobbyists that was threatening the government. In particular, Wilson complained about the "extraordinary exertions" that lobbyists were making to kill his efforts to reform tariffs.

"The government, which was designed for the people, has got into the hands of the bosses and their employers, the special interests," Wilson said. "An invisible empire has been set up above the forms of democracy." An "Invisible Empire." Cosa Nostra is designed to be an "invisible, and secret Empire." One that is an enemy of the government, not an Empire invited to do business with.

Wilson was able to tamp down opposition to his tariff reforms and send the "insidious" lobbyists scurrying to the shadows. But as the US recovered from the Great Depression, government spending increased dramatically, and lobbyists reemerged to help the clients figure out how to make money off government programs like the Tennessee Valley Authority, collective bargaining, the Glass–Steagall banking act, the Public Works Administration, and other New Deal programs. Former insiders—retired elected officials and their political aides—discovered a lucrative niche in the world of influence. Tommy Corcoran, one of FDR's top aides and a New Deal architect, left government to become a lobbyist helping special interests benefit from all the new government programs.

Business Gets the Memo

The real explosion in lobbying came about fifty years later when business executives, drowning in regulations and taxes inflicted on them by a growing federal government, said enough was enough.

Their frustration was captured in a memo written by a corporate lawyer named Lewis F. Powell in 1971. Powell, who would go on to be a Supreme Court justice, raged about how the country's business interests were under attack from the government and special interests.

"Few elements of American society today have as little influence in government as the American businessman, the corporation, or even the millions of corporate stockholders," Powell wrote.

Business executives were tired of guys like Ralph Nader painting them as heartless profit machines whose toys, vehicles, and appliances were shoddy and dangerous, whose plants were spewing pollution, and whose workers were pummeled by low wages and deplorable working conditions. Nader talked lawmakers into tighter environmental regulations, fewer trade protections, and higher taxes.

To fight back, corporations invested—first in conservative think tanks like the Cato Institute and the Heritage Foundation, then in lobbying. The think tanks helped reshape the public view about the role of business in creating jobs, and the lobbyists killed a major labor reform bill, got several costly federal regulations rolled back, negotiated reduced corporate taxes, and convinced an increasing number of Americans that we all needed less government regulation in our lives and our economy. What started out with honorable intentions was soon corrupted as greedy government officials learned how to use lobbying as a way to enrich themselves.

Business never backed off after that. By one account, it spends thirty-four dollars on lobbying for every dollar spent by unions or public interest groups. Corporate lobbyists are embedded in Congressional staff. They provide data, polling information, white papers, and policy recommendations that Hill staffers depend on to create new regulations or revise policies. As a result, when times get tough—as they periodically do in a capitalist economy—the government is less likely to respond with New Deal solutions than it is with bailouts, tax cuts, and faith that creating jobs and helping businesses that are "too big to fail" will guide us through the dark times.

Lobbying really changed how business leaders viewed politics. Lobbying, they figured out, didn't just protect profits by keeping taxes and regulations down. It also was a source of new profits. This is exactly how the Mafia operates too.

Lobbying as an Economic Issue

Lobbying today isn't what most people think it is. We think of people in sharp suits buying politicians lunch and donating to their campaigns in return for fat government contracts. That happens, but the control lobbyists have over our government is much more significant than that. Lobbyists have learned the ways of the street.

Economists call it "rent-seeking." It's a bad term because it has nothing to do with rent as most of us know it. Instead, rent-seeking is when a special interest convinces a policymaker to adjust a regulation to benefit the special interest's profits. The benefit might come in the form of a subsidy, market monopolies, a favorable tax bracket, tariffs that discourage foreign competition, and tighter regulations that make it difficult for new competitors to break into the market. That last one really makes my blood boil. That's what we did on the street. We got rid of our competitor by any means necessary. Government officials are not supposed to give an unfair advantage to anyone that plays that game. But they do and all too often. And they don't do it without it benefiting them.

A good example is how car dealers tried to prevent Tesla from getting a foothold in local markets. Tesla wanted to cut out the middleman and sell directly to customers, so car-dealer lobbyists worked to strengthen state laws that require cars be sold through dealerships. Car dealers argued that dealership regulations make it more convenient for the consumer. Buyers can comparison shop more easily, and the dealerships offer more consumer protection. To make sure state policymakers understood, the dealers made nearly a million dollars in campaign contributions in New Jersey alone. Campaign contributions, meaning bribes, to curry favor with the elected official.

This is a classic example of rent-seeking. But it's also a classic example of Mob behavior. The carmakers didn't have to spend money to come up with a product that would compete better than Tesla. They didn't have to cut their own profits in order to compete. They didn't have to innovate or increase efficiency. All they had to do was "lobby" lawmakers and make campaign contributions. Tesla still can't sell its cars in some states as a result.

How the Consumer Loses

Tesla was not the only loser in this scenario. You and I also lose. We don't get the lower prices and better selection that free-market competition brings.

For another prime example of how lawmakers benefit themselves at the public's expense, look at how Big Pharma influenced Medicare. Pharmaceutical companies have always hated the idea of the government adding a drug benefit to Medicare. That would give the government an opportunity to purchase in bulk. Bulk pricing lowers the drugmaker's profits. So in 2000, when Medicare Part D was introduced, pharmaceutical lobbyists managed to get a regulation introduced that ensured government funding for medication but forbade bulk purchasing. The result was a $205 billion benefit to drug companies—and higher prices for consumers. When our elected officials allow drug companies to compromise our ability to get pharmaceuticals at a price that is more cost-effective to consumers who need them to maintain their health, that's Mob-like behavior. It's despicable when people can't afford medication because the government allows pricing that benefits the lawmakers themselves. How many lives are seriously compromised because of the outrageous prices for drugs? Trump tried to remedy this but was up against too much opposition.

Ever wonder why conservatives, including Donald Trump, were never able to rescind Obamacare? There were a lot of factors, but one of the biggest was this fact: If the Affordable Care Act were repealed, insurance companies would lose $1 trillion. The insurance industry's $150-million-a-year lobbying army would never sit still for that.

Rent-seeking occurs and businesses invest in it because our elected officials let them get away with it. As a result, we pay more for stuff and we have fewer choices. What's more, the money the government gives up every time it reduces corporate taxes or provides some industry a government giveaway is money that the government can't spend on things the rest of us need, like safe roads or better schools.

Marvin Ammori, a fellow at the New America Foundation, calls this a "corruption economy" because firms compete for influence rather than innovation. According to the Center for American Progress, businesses that lobby or make campaign contributions get the highest payoffs from favorable policy decisions. Economists agree this practice hurts the overall economy.

Why would businesses want to hurt the economy? Because they have no choice. It's the way our elected leaders have fashioned the game. If an industry is to survive today, they have to have a luxurious seat at the lobbying table. If they aren't there, their competitors surely will be, and they might find their business struggling to turn a profit against the better rent-seekers as a result. One study found that increasing lobbying reduces a corporation's effective tax rate. Another study found that each $1 campaign contribution on the state level is worth $6.65 in lower state corporate taxes. Lobbying provides a great return. It keeps shareholders happy.

Make no mistake; elected officials created this lobbying system for their own personal benefit. The system keeps the flow of money moving—whether it's campaign contributions, special perks, or straight-out payoffs. The Mafia Commission case was all about my former associates extorting money from cement contractors in New York in return for large construction contracts and labor peace. In this case, the government is extorting money from big-corporation lobbyists.

Ironically, all this lobbying actually results in *more* government regulation—the exact opposite of what Powell saw as a benefit of corporate lobbying fifty years ago. That's because lobbyist-backed bills are more complex and confusing than bills not backed by special interests. It's easier to hide lucrative side deals when you tuck them into a two-thousand-page law. In California, group-sponsored bills are usually about 30 percent longer than non sponsored bills.

"The complexity and incoherence of our government often make it difficult for us to understand just what the government is doing," Steven Teles, a political scientist at Johns Hopkins and the coauthor of *The Captured Economy*, wrote. "And among the practices it most frequently hides from view is the growing tendency of public policy to redistribute resources upward to the wealthy and the organized at the expense of the poorer and less organized."

Lobbying works so well that big corporations now lobby other countries. Consider China, for example. A lot of US companies moved there to take advantage of the cheap labor. But when the Chinese considered improving workers' rights, the American Chamber of Commerce and the European Union Chamber of Commerce applied lobbying pressure to reduce worker benefits. The US Food Lobby—led by Coca-Cola, McDonalds, and KFC—hasn't been content to just open restaurants in Europe and China. It's also wormed its way onto policymaking bodies in many countries to ensure governments don't try to control their obesity epidemics by reducing guidelines for sugar and saturated fat.

Again, lobbying has direct parallels to how the Mob operates. When I got involved in skimming gas taxes in the early 1980s, the only way I was able to get the wholesale licenses I needed was through political connections. Instead of outright bribing, I developed relationships with politicians. I got to know them, and they got to know me. Through my fundraising efforts, I became important to them. I helped keep them in office, and in return, they got me all the licenses I needed.

Likewise, when you're dealing with a Mafia Democracy, strong arguments aren't enough. You have to sweeten the pot.

Changing the System

The first step in changing the "corruption economy" would be to put a freeze on allowing people in public office to leave government and immediately join a lobbying firm. We see this too often. A politician or Hill staffer should not be allowed to leave the government and immediately go to work for the same industry that he regulated while in office. When that happens, how can you not conclude that the politician is getting a nice, fat payoff for helping that industry while in office?

A surprising number of politicians retire from office and stay in Washington, DC. In 2018, thirty-six members of the House and Senate decided not to run for reelection, the most since 1992. Of the forty-eight lawmakers who left office after 2016, one in four stayed in Washington to work as a lawyer or lobbyist or to join a lobbyist-supported think tank. For many, their new jobs are a lot like their old jobs: they take meetings and walk the halls of Congress, prodding their former colleagues to support whatever industry they now represent. Among those who left office after the 2014 midterms, about half stayed within the Beltway. According to one analysis by the *Atlantic Monthly*, ex-lawmakers can cash in mightily by joining the influence business, with many earning three times their $174,000 Congressional base salary.

It wasn't always this way. According to a study at Georgia State and Exeter University, only a handful of retired politicians became lobbyists in the 1970s when Powell's "Attack on Free Enterprise" manifesto rocked the business world. By 2006, about 40 percent of the 200 House members who left office in the preceding years registered as lobbyists. They came from both parties. Famous pols like Tom Foley and Newt Gingrich cashed in big time. So did Tom Daschle, George Mitchell, Trent Lott, and Bob Dole.

The exodus and the unsavory quid-pro-quo optics convinced Congress to enact a one-year "cooling off" period barring recently retired politicians from lobbying their former coworkers. But all that did was lead to a practice called "shadow lobbying." That's when a former lawmaker goes to work for a lobbying firm but never registers as a lobbyist. They design lobbying campaigns, develop messaging, and identify the targets, but they don't take face-to-face meetings. Gingrich and former Rep. John Boehner took that route.

Presidents have vowed to ban lobbyists from their administrations. Obama signed an executive order prohibiting lobbyists in his administration from working on issues they used to support as lobbyists, but he stepped back from prohibiting former lawmakers from lobbying the White House. Trump made his appointees sign a pledge swearing they wouldn't accept gifts from lobbyists, but the rule wasn't enforced, and nearly two hundred lobbyists swarmed to the White House to take jobs with his administration, according to ProPublica.

After beating Trump in the 2020 election, Joe Biden immediately faced criticism when lobbyists wormed their way into jobs with the new administration. Liberal groups implored Biden to reconsider, calling many of his advisors "corporatists." But Biden said he didn't want to rule out individuals with deep expertise on key issues, like healthcare, and some of those knowledgeable individuals have worked as lobbyists. Biden's former chief of staff, Steve Richetti, was a lobbyist for the big-spending pharmaceutical industry, as well as for insurance companies and credit agencies. Richetti's brother operates a lobbying firm that started signing up new clients soon after Biden began leading in the polls in his campaign against Trump. Is it any surprise, when Biden mandated that so many Americans get the COVID vaccine? Could it be that his own people were helping their former clients by increasing demand for vaccines? These are the questions people need to ask. Demand answers. Demand transparency.

Let the Sun Shine In

I'm not saying that people with an interest in business should be banned from talking to lawmakers. We all have First Amendment rights and the right to petition our government.

But I am suggesting that if our elected leaders are cutting deals with lobbyists, there should be a public record of what was said and agreed to. Let's open up the process so people like you and me can read about what's going on behind closed doors. Working with lobbyists is not "classified information" that needs to be kept hidden from the public due to security concerns. Lobbyists dealing with elected officials are more like Mob "sit-downs" where nefarious business deals are being discussed and transacted. Just because the government officials make the lobbying system "legal" doesn't make it right. It certainly doesn't ensure the practice is in the best interest of the people the government officials swear to serve. Once again, a Mafia Democracy at work.

Obama sort of had the right approach with his ethics rules from 2009. He not only banned registered lobbyists from working in agencies they had once tried to influence, but he ordered the White House to release a list of all visitors so the public could see which corporate executives and lobbyists were meeting with the president or his staff. No president had ever done that before.

The problem with Obama's approach was that it didn't go far enough. The records were not very detailed, and they weren't released until three or four months after everything was already said and done. The records were only kept for the White House, not for Congress, which is where all the real sausage is made anyway.

We need Congress to take this same approach. The way it's done now—secret deals, payoffs, money stashed in freezers—that's Mafia behavior. It's Machiavellian. It's not what our founders envisioned. Our founders pictured honest citizens asking for help, like the colonel from the Revolutionary War trying to get back pay for his fellow soldiers. James Madison foresaw factions making appeals to Congress, but he didn't anticipate the corrupt economy and the underhanded backroom deals we see (or don't see) today.

Lobbying issues need to be made public, and negotiations between Hill staffers and lobbyists have to be open to the public—or at least part of the public record. There needs to be a transcript of meetings, and those transcripts need to be freely available. The more things are open and scrutinized, the less inclined people are going to be to do the wrong thing.

We also need to close the revolving door on retired lawmakers moving to K Street and K Street lobbyists slipping into federal policymaking roles. Ironically, lobbying has become such a big issue that nonprofits have formed to fight it. There's only one hitch; if you want to work for the anti-lobbying Common Cause or The Revolving Door Project, you may have to register as a lobbyist.

Chapter 3

Campaign Spending and Corruption

"When plunder becomes a way of life for a group of men in a society, over the course of time they create for themselves a legal system that authorizes it and a moral code that glorifies it."

—FREDERIC BASTIAT

THE INK WASN'T DRY ON THE CONSTITUTION WHEN SPE-cial interests started showing up at the back door of Congress with bags of money and requests for special favors.

William Maclay, a US senator from Pennsylvania, complained about bribery, insider trading on government deliberations, and other chicanery in the diary he kept from 1789–1791. A few years later, a senator from Tennessee named William Blount was expelled from Congress after going into debt and conspiring with the British to take over West Florida. During President Andrew Jackson's presidency, one of his appointees to the New York City Collector's Office embezzled $1.2 million before fleeing to Europe to avoid prosecution.

In 1857, US Representative Orsamus Matteson, a New York Republican, announced that most of his House colleagues were "purchasable." Then Matteson himself was accused of accepting bribes to support a Minnesota land bill.

As time went on, the scandals became more elaborate and the corruption more widespread. Some of the skullduggery was straight out of the Mafia handbook. From 1864 to 1867, the Union Pacific Railroad set up a fraudulent company and greatly inflated the construction costs for the First Transcontinental Railroad. Railroad executives billed the federal government $94 million for a $50 million construction project and then used some of the $44 million windfall to bribe several officeholders for bills, grants, and regulations that favored the railroad.

The railroad scam damaged the public's faith in their elected leaders, and nothing that happened in the ensuing forty years did anything to change that. Finally, in 1907, President Teddy Roosevelt signed into law the Tillman Act, the nation's first campaign finance law. It prohibited federal politicians from taking money from corporations or interstate banks. Roosevelt didn't want private money to influence lawmaking or to buy elections, although Roosevelt himself had accepted plenty of corporate donations in his campaign for the 1904 election.

You might think that the bad guys were the corporate bagmen buying favors from politicians. But ironically, corporations were all in favor of the new bill prohibiting them from funding campaigns. Why? Because they were tired of elected officials demanding contributions in return for favorable treatment.

At the turn of the twentieth century, national parties funded campaigns, and the parties had no qualms about hitting up rich corporations for money. In the 1896 election, for example, President McKinley's chief fundraiser, Mark Hanna, made calculated and precise demands for contributions. He hit up Standard Oil for $250,000. He asked banks to give a quarter of 1 percent of their capital. When requesting donations, Hanna made a point of listing how much the potential donor's competitors had already given him. It was a classic shakedown.

Roosevelt institutionalized this form of government extortion. In the lead-up to the 1904 election, Roosevelt put his secretary of commerce and labor, George Cortelyou, in charge of the Republican National Committee. In other words, the guy in charge of investigating corporations was also going around asking those corporations for donations. It was a textbook example of conflict of interest.

Not surprisingly, corporate America was "entranced with happiness" when the Tillman Act was passed.

"We welcome this legislation with very much the same emotions with which a serf would his liberation from a tyrannous autocrat," said one financial figure at the time.

The *New York Times* also praised the Tillman Act.

"[The act] will lessen a very mean and sordid practice of blackmail," the newspaper wrote in a 1907 editorial. "The great number of corporations that have suffered extortion through weakness and cowardice will have their backbones stiffened, and parties will be put to it to fill their coffers by really a voluntary contributions."

Sadly, nothing changed. After the Tillman Act, several other campaign finance laws arrived over the next century, but Congress never learned how to resist the lure of corporate riches. The amount of money has increased and the flow of transactions between corporations and Congress is even more opaque than it was in Roosevelt's time.

As a former Mob boss, I know what extortion looks like. We did it all the time. In return for regular payments, we would promise to protect your business from harm. Those who didn't pay found that the harm arrived fairly quickly. Nobody would mention that the protectors are also the antagonists, but that was understood.

And politicians understand it better than we did.

Expensive Campaigns

These days, it costs a fortune to run for office and win an election. According to the Center for Responsive Politics, 2020 spending on presidential and congressional races reached nearly $11 billion, shattering the all-time record. Four years earlier, the cost was $7 billion. The $5.6 billion spent on House and Senate campaigns in 2020 was 37 percent higher than the 2016 campaign.

In the old days, politicians reached voters by standing on tree stumps or giving speeches from the back of a railroad car. As our country grew, it became necessary to spend more to reach more people. At first, politicians cozied up with newspaper publishers to get their message out, and later they started running television ads. Dwight Eisenhower was the first presidential candidate to advertise on TV, and Lyndon Johnson was the first to employ negative advertising when he aired the "Daisy Girl" ad in 1964. That sixty-second commercial depicted a three-year-old plucking petals from a daisy while a nuclear blast went off, suggesting that Johnson's Republican opponent, Barry Goldwater, was the genocidal maniac who flipped the switch. Goldwater lost in a landslide.

The size and complexity of modern elections force our politicians to constantly raise money. It never stops, particularly for House members who face reelection every two years. The time consumed campaigning and fundraising is staggering. And it's getting worse. Whereas Ronald Reagan, who won presidential elections in 1980 and 1984, attended 8 campaign fundraisers in his two terms, Barack Obama attended 228.

Politicians' need for huge campaign coffers ensures that they will appeal to wealthy individuals and rich corporations. In the 2012 election cycle, for instance, political action committees distributed more than $1 billion—73 percent of which came from only one hundred people. The result is a warped system in which rich people determine who gets to run, who gets elected, and what the officeholders' legislative agenda will be. In this sense, Al Capone was right when he said, "Capitalism is the legitimate racket of the ruling class." I couldn't agree more.

Both parties are guilty. In 2015, the billionaire Koch brothers brought together a group of big spenders for a retreat in Palm Springs, California. There, they unveiled a plan to raise and spend $1 billion dollars before the primaries started, giving the group unprecedented influence over who the likely Republican candidate would be. Ted Cruz, Marco Rubio, and Rand Paul all showed up to chat and stick out their hands. Democrats like George Soros and Tom Steyer also dole out millions to progressive candidates, giving the two of them an outsized influence over elections.

Dependence Corruption

None of this rises to the level of corruption, but it violates the spirit of the Constitution. As Madison noted in the Federalist Papers, the framers of the Constitution intended Congress to be "dependent on the people alone." But that is not happening. If politicians were dependent on average citizens, they'd be tackling social issues like reliable internet that everyone can tap into, daycare, affordable banking that gets poor people out from under the thumb of predatory lenders, and immigration reform. Instead, our politicians focus on federal regulations, tariffs, and other business-related issues that are important to their corporate benefactors.

Political scientists call this *dependence corruption*. According to Lawrence Lessig of Harvard Law School, dependence corruption occurs when a political institution stops operating under "the proper influences." Instead, the politicians bow to contributors and lobbyists.

Dependence corruption isn't bribery or *quid pro quo* transactions but is instead based on giving and receiving political favors. An example is when the chairman of the House of Armed Services Committee sends fundraiser invitations to defense contractors. That kind of thing happens so often in Congress that no one even bothers to squawk about it. Do you think the contractor is going to turn down the invite? Or is that contractor going to try to buy more tickets to the event than their competitor? Of course they are, and the politician knows it.

A great example of dependence corruption occurred in 2009 when the House Financial Services Committee invited the CEOs of several big financial institutions to testify about how they were spending billions of dollars in taxpayer-funded bailout money.

This was at the height of The Great Recession. Banks had nearly triggered a Depression by making crappy and risky subprime loans and then packaging and reselling them. When those unqualified borrowers stopped making their house payments, the economic collapse was rapid and widespread. Even those of us who continued paying our mortgages and monthly bills took a punch to the solar plexus as our retirement accounts were decimated and our neighbors lost their homes, jobs, and businesses.

And in the middle of this historic period of desperation, the greedy masterminds of this collapse were testifying before the people we elected to represent us. The average guy tuning in to C-SPAN may have expected these insanely rich, tailored bankers to get invited to the woodshed.

Didn't happen.

In fact, the lawmakers seemed almost…*deferential* to these Wall Street shysters. Why?

For starters, virtually every member of the committee had received campaign contributions from these same financial institutions the year before. What's more, according to the Center for Responsive Politics, eighteen of the committee's members had personal investments in the financial institutions whose CEOs were testifying. These companies' PACs and employees had donated nearly $11 million to Congress in 2008. The hot seat we thought these CEOs were in was only lukewarm, the center observed. The politicians had come to rely on the bankers' political support, and this gave the bankers incredible leverage over the lawmakers. The bankers held a financial gun to the politicians' heads, and as Al Capone once noted, "You can get much further with a kind word and a gun than you can with a kind word alone."

In truth, the CEOs and elected officials on the House Financial Services Committee weren't adversaries. They were partners. They were coconspirators. They relied on each other—the congressmen for campaign money and the CEOs for the billions in free money they needed to correct their mistakes. What a life!

What's more, when politicians and policy experts leave Washington, many go to work at places like Goldman Sachs. When the government needs help writing financial regulations, they recruit executives from places like Goldman Sachs. It's a revolving door. It's why Capitol Hill is often referred to as "Government Sachs."

According to Richard Painter, the chief White House ethics lawyer in the George W. Bush administration, watching these corrupt financiers mooch off the people they helped put in office was a "national humiliation." In fact, Painter said, this demonstration of dependence corruption "in a supposedly free economy" is what inspired the Tea Party movement. People were disgusted.

"The financial industry's campaign contributions and the incessant revolving door between Wall Street and Washington…alienated ordinary Americans who paid their own debts," Painter wrote in his book *Taxation Only with Representation*. "The founders did not intend it to be this way."

Neither did the general public. In a 2018 survey by the Pew Research Center, Americans overwhelmingly supported limits on political campaign spending. Voters from both parties agreed that people who make big campaign contributions should not have more political influence than others.

Getting around the Law

The Tillman Act didn't change anything, and neither did the federal Corrupt Practices Act, which requires politicians and parties to disclose all money spent on elections, or the Federal Election Campaign Act, which was passed and amended after the Watergate scandal. Congress created the Federal Election Commission to put some teeth in the regulation, but the commission is purposely weak and ineffective. Every time politicians decide they are going to do something about the high costs of campaigns and the influence money pouring in from special interests, the problem only gets worse. Why is that?

It's Machiavellian, that's why. Congress passes laws to keep rich corporate donors out of campaigns so politicians can pretend they truly want to stem the flow of cash. But in truth and action, politicians don't want to change anything. All the laws do is create new mechanisms—soft money, PACs, super PACs, dark money, and secretive nonprofits that raise billions and don't have to say who their contributors are.

Elected officials are more two-faced about campaign contributions than about any other major issue. Despite the Tillman Act, guys like Bill Clinton continued to solicit money from corporations, claiming the money was for "generic party-building." Clinton claimed to be in favor of campaign finance reform, yet during his reelection campaign, he would invite big donors to spend the night at the White House in the Lincoln bedroom.

Obama was one of the biggest hypocrites. Obama denounced super PACs, which can accept donations of unlimited size but have to reveal the names of their donors and regularly disclose their activity. But by 2012, Obama allies had set up a super PAC to help with his reelection. This also made me think of Machiavelli, who once said, "It is necessary for a prince wishing to hold his own to know how to do wrong, and to make use of it or not according to necessity."

When court decisions paved the way for nonprofits that can raise billions without having to disclose their "dark money" donors, the Democrats pretended to be appalled by the new practice. They vowed not to participate in the new game.

"Unless a bright light is shined on the shadowy activity of these outside groups, people aren't going to know the facts, which is that with their complete lack of transparency, Lord knows who's participated in these races," said Obama spokesman Bill Burton. "And the president thinks that if you're going to participate in politics, you ought to be transparent about it."

Sounds good. Sounds honest. Let the sun shine in!

Six months later, Obama set up his own secretive fundraising machinery, whose goal was to raise $100 million for Obama's reelection. The guy in charge? Bill Burton.

Again, that's Mafia behavior. It's Machiavellian: "Whosoever desires constant success must change his conduct with the times."

Obama's tune changed when he saw how much conservatives were raising through these secretive nonprofits. From 2004 to 2012, the amount of dark money in campaigns climbed from $5.9 million to more than $300 million. From 2008 to 2014, nine of the top ten dark money spenders were Republican, led by Karl Rove's Crossroads GPS group, which raised and spent $142 million for conservative campaigns. The Democrats couldn't take it anymore. By 2018, they were raising more dark money than the Republicans.

Joe Biden has already shown he's as much of a hypocrite as Obama when it comes to campaign finance. While publicly disavowing super PACs in 2019, he was privately signaling his willingness to start one for his campaign. His justification? The only way to stop the corrupt practices of Donald Trump was through the, well, corrupt practice of accepting huge donations himself.

"It's just like everything else Biden stands for. He believes it until it's of political benefit to reverse himself," said Trump campaign communications director Tim Murtaugh.

The result of all this is that since 2010, when the Supreme Court's *Citizens United* ruling paved the way for politically active nonprofits, dark money groups have spent about a billion dollars on television and online advertising and mailers to influence elections. And this arms race is only accelerating: According to OpenSecrets.org, the Center for Responsive Politics' online database of campaign spending, in 2016 conservatives had four times as much dark money as Democrats—$144 million to $38 million. But by 2018, Democrats were outspending the Republicans.

And for the most part, we don't know where that money is coming from. It could be coming from foreign governments.

"People could use the dark pools of our campaign finance system to decide who runs our government and how the government wields its power, with potentially massive ramifications for our national security and independence," said Painter, the former White House ethics lawyer.

But there are also massive ramifications for US citizens, who are increasingly being cut out of elections and the political process and asked to pay the price for the favors politicians owe their benefactors. We can't afford to disregard the importance of this or write it off as "politics as usual." It's Machiavellian. It's wrong, and we're all paying the price.

Foreign Influence

The thing that scares me most about our weak campaign finance laws is this threat posed by foreign governments. Everyone made a big deal about Russia's shenanigans on social media in the 2016 elections, but the truth is that there is nothing new about foreign governments trying to pick our officeholders. They've been doing that for years, and it's only getting easier for them.

In the old days, when the United States was the world's only superpower, there wasn't much to worry about. Most of the countries who had economic interests in our country were our friends and allies.

Today, it's different. The US is just one of several economic superpowers. Trade barriers have gone down, and foreign companies have tremendous investments in our country. Foreign nationals own resorts, high-rise towers, and meat-processing facilities. They own a big chunk of our national debt. And foreign investments in the US are only increasing. In 2008, foreign investments totaled about $2 trillion. Five years later, it had climbed to $2.7 trillion. By 2020, foreign direct investments totaled $4.5 trillion.

Companies from China, Russia, Europe, and the Middle East have a lot of skin in the American game. Does anyone really think that with so much at stake these companies aren't paying attention to who gets elected? Does anyone think the Chinese aren't as interested in rent-seeking as General Electric or General Motors? *P. 65*

Although the US amended the Federal Election Campaign Act in 1966 to ban campaign contributions from foreign governments and foreign nationals, we've already documented how easy it is to get around it. And it may be even easier for foreign operators to influence local issues.

In 2015, when Los Angeles County was considering a ballot measure that required porn stars to wear condoms during filming, the German founder of a huge porn-distribution company was suspected of funneling hundreds of thousands of dollars to fight the measure. The referendum passed, but an AIDS advocacy group complained to the Federal Election Commission (FEC) that the German mogul had illegally pumped (sorry) $327,000 into the campaign to defeat it. The FEC, divided by the three Democrats who favored an investigation and three Republicans opposed to it, declined to pursue the case.

This wasn't an isolated case. The year before, a Mexican contractor was accused of funneling at least $500,000 to super PACs because he wanted to support Southern California politicians in a position to help him develop the San Diego waterfront.

Foreign powers are also contributing heavily to Washington,

DC, think tanks. These think tanks, many of which hire former politicians when they leave office, hold tremendous sway over government policy. Although some think tanks are conservative and some are more progressive, their work is often considered to be nonpartisan and objective, and their studies are often the impetus for federal policy decisions.

But in 2014, the *New York Times* reported that more than a dozen prominent research groups received tens of millions of dollars from foreign governments to adopt policies the donors favored. The think tanks aren't required to divulge where their money comes from, but some scholars admitted they are pressured to make findings that favor their funders. Think tank executives disputed those charges—"Our currency is our credibility," said one chief executive—but an internal report commissioned by the Norwegian Foreign Affairs Ministry suggested otherwise: "Think tanks in Washington are openly conveying that they can service only those foreign governments that provide funding," the report said.

Since 2011 at least sixty-four foreign governments have given nearly $100 million to twenty-eight think thanks. The United Arab Emirates gave the Center for Strategic and International Studies a million dollars to build the center's new glass-and-steel headquarters down the street from the White House. Qatar forked over $14.8 million to the Brookings Institute, which is a nonprofit public policy think tank in Washington, DC.

And the return on the foreign investment in think tanks goes beyond a typical white paper filled with bar charts and tables. The think tanks insist that they don't lobby elected officials, but the truth is they do. The Center for Global Development, for example, got money from Norway and then went to the White House and Congress to lobby on the country's behalf.

Foreign interests do plenty of direct lobbying too. According to the Center for Responsive Politics, American subsidiaries of foreign companies can legally form PACs and collect contributions from their employees. In 2014, these groups raised more than $14 million.

What's happening is that our leaders are putting America up for sale to foreign governments. In the name of greed, our elected leaders are opening the door to our enemies. It has to stop.

Why We Must Correct This

The problems I've outlined in this chapter show how little influence most of us regular citizens have. Government is supposed to be there to serve us, not Qatar, Norway, or a contractor from Mexico. Our government is supposed to be elected by us, not by Russia or China or some other emerging world economic power. But as campaigns grow increasingly and insanely expensive, our elected officials become more reliant on big donors. Those donors, whether they are corrupt financiers from Wall Street or foreign powers like China, are supplanting us. They are drowning us out.

What's more, these lobbyists, super PACs, and dark-money nonprofits are causing our government to expand. Regulations proliferate, profiting corporations with money to hire K Street lobbyists but strangling the rest of us. Regulations are the cudgel politicians hold over the heads of corporations who don't contribute to their campaigns. These are classic Mafia extortion tactics. Campaign contributions encourage more waste, more spending on earmarks, and more contracts for equipment the government doesn't need or use. If you're a religious conservative and you want your government to talk about abortion, gambling, pornography, and euthanasia, forget about it; you can't be heard. These are issues that affect our lives and our families, and our opinions on them are falling on deaf ears.

In its 2010 *Citizens United* decision, the Supreme Court equated corporate wealth with free political speech. To stop corporations from funding campaigns is to deprive them of their First Amendment free speech rights. But free speech for who? For China? We are in a global economy where corporate wealth in America is no longer restricted to US citizens, so the effect of the court decision was to throw open the door for wealthy foreign nationals and oligarchs to waltz in and manipulate our elective bodies. This is so dangerous.

This should be a nonpartisan issue. Each side of the aisle points to the other side and says, "I have to raise all this money because the other party is doing it!" Let's cut the bullshit.

Republicans have to remember the great words of conservative stalwarts like John McCain and Barry Goldwater. "In order to achieve the widest possible distribution of political power, financial contributions to political campaigns should be made by individuals and individuals alone," Goldwater said. "I see no reason for labor unions—or corporations—to participate in politics."

And the Democrats have to stop talking out of both sides of their mouths, condemning soaring election costs and campaign fundraising one day and launching super PACs the next. They're always claiming they want to take the high road but can't because of the greedy Republicans. This, too, is bullshit. It's also the epitome of hypocrisy.

The Downside of Greed

Again, the Mafia's experience serves as a cautionary tale of what happens when greed and growth make you lose sight of your values.

For almost twenty-five years leading up to the 1970s, the Mafia's Commission had "closed the books" on bringing in new inductees. If someone died or was killed, the family would be able to replace him. But for the most part, less was more because the Mafia wanted to remain discreet and closed off from outside influences.

That all changed when other criminal organizations started moving into our territory in the 1970s and 1980s. To increase their cash flow and control, the bosses increased the ranks of the soldiers paying them tribute. The Mob's security and secrecy soon suffered.

During my time in the Mob, the Mafia's ranks in New York swelled to approximately 750 to 800 made men. Each one of those guys had a number of associates. I had more than 300 associates, including members of the Russian Mob I had recruited into my organization, so the total number for all the families had to be in the tens of thousands. We made money hand over fist with everything from concrete and garbage to gas and gambling.

But the Mob's run of prosperity did not last. The bosses soon learned that bigger is not always better. When the Justice Department started their RICO investigations, they had no problem finding Mob associates willing to rat out their partners to stay out of jail. The Mob's ethos of *omerta* had been diluted by our rapid expansion. Some who were caught in the RICO net kept their mouths shut, but for the most part, our sense of honor and secrecy had been destroyed.

When any organization, criminal or otherwise, becomes so big and exerts so much control over another body of people, a majority of those people will suffer. Money and power can be intoxicating in the hands of the wrong people. The bigger an organization, the harder it is to police its members. Corruption within its ranks is inevitable.

Mafia Organizational Chart

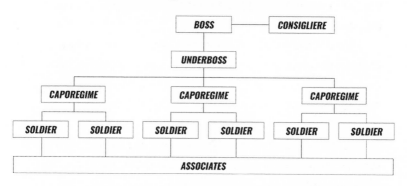

U.S. Government Organizational Chart

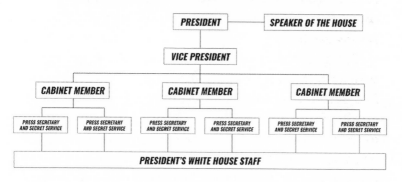

And that's what we're seeing in the halls of Congress and in statehouses across the country. For too many politicians, the measure of their success isn't how many bills they can pass but how much money they can raise for their reelection. They've opened the floodgates to big donors, just like the Mob did, and now, just like the Mob, they have gone too far.

But, as we'll learn in the next chapter, the flood of campaign dollars that has corrupted the national pride we once felt in our republic is just the tip of the iceberg. Read on to find out how politicians blatantly use their office to openly enrich themselves through unethical practices.

Chapter 4

How Politicians Enrich Themselves

"Poverty wants some things, Luxury many things, Avarice all things."

—BENJAMIN FRANKLIN

RICHARD BURR WAS NOT A RICH MAN. HE WAS A SALES manager for a lawn equipment company in 1994 when he was first elected to the House of Representatives as a Republican from North Carolina. In 2004, he was elected to the Senate. During most of his Senate career, his estimated net worth was around $1.5 million, below the median net worth of all senators.

That changed in 2015, shortly after Burr rose to become the chair of the powerful Senate Intelligence Committee. According to data compiled by OpenSecrets.org, Burr's wealth soared as his stature in the Senate rose, with his estimated net worth skyrocketing to $7.3 million. This was a guy making less than $175,000 a year.

How did he do it? Part of the reason was that Burr, like so

many of his colleagues in the Senate, somehow became a brilliant investor. As a senator, he suddenly began making stock trades with uncanny skill and timing.

Burr's stock-trading skills were on full display in February 2020 when, as chairman of the Intelligence Committee, he received a private briefing on the coronavirus. The virus was spreading fast, he learned, and would likely have a dramatic effect on the US and its economy. People would lose their jobs, companies would close, and travel would have to be severely restricted. Hundreds of thousands might die from COVID-19.

Shortly after the briefing, Burr unloaded up to $1.7 million in stock he held in hotel chains, including Wyndham Hotels and Resorts and Extended Stay America.

A week later, as the public became more fully aware of the dangers posed by the virus, the stock market plummeted, losing 30 percent of its value. The stock price for Wyndham declined by more than 60 percent, and shares in Extended Stay dropped 50 percent. Burr's timely trades had saved him a small fortune.

On the same day Burr made his trades, his brother-in-law, Gerald Fauth, a former lobbyist and a Trump appointee to the three-person National Mediation Board, ditched nearly $300,000 in stocks he held in companies that would later be hit hard by the pandemic. According to a Manhattan investigative firm that examined the trades, Fauth avoided as much as $118,000 in losses by selling when he did.

Was it insider trading—which is a crime for ordinary citizens? Burr denied that it was, but the timing of the trades—coming on the heels of the early warnings he received as a privileged senator—suggest otherwise.

Both Sides of His Mouth

What was more clear was Burr's willingness to say one thing while believing something else entirely.

At the same time he was scrambling to unload his stocks, Burr was telling the rest of us that there was no reason to panic. Everything was going to be okay. He even wrote an op-ed piece for Fox News declaring that the US was "better prepared than ever before" to control the virus. Relax, people. HYPOCRISY! I'm not sure even a Mob guy would stoop this low. A politician who lies to the public for their own financial benefit is equally criminal. It makes me sick.

Immediately after Burr's op-ed was published and his self-serving stock transactions were completed, Burr changed his tune. This time he told a small gathering of wealthy members of the nonpartisan Tar Heel Club that the virus was "more aggressive in its transmission than anything we have seen in recent history." He told company leaders that they "may have to alter…travel" and consider using video conferencing instead of physical travel. What Burr told the public was much different from what he told his wealthy friends. Is this not criminal? People would soon start dying in droves, and Burr knew it. Yet he downplayed the risks to improve his own wealth. How many people died because they believed people like Burr, who said there was little risk from the virus? Obviously, a false statement. A lie. Why? Well, for personal gain, obviously, but there may have been other reasons for lying. As John Gotti once said, "I never lie to any man because I don't fear anyone. The only time you lie is when you are afraid." What was Burr afraid of?

Burr's two-faced behavior is typical. His use of insider knowledge to avoid big losses on the stock market is also typical—just one more way politicians exploit their privileged positions to enrich themselves. So many politicians use insider trading to get rich that it's almost part of their job description. They get a private briefing about a deadly disease, pending legislation, secret merger talks, or a looming financial crisis, and they scurry back to their office to make their trades before the word gets out.

You see it again and again. After the coronavirus briefing, Sen. Diane Feinstein, James Inhofe, and Kelly Loeffler also raced back to the Hill to make trades. Feinstein unloaded up to $6 million in stock in a biotech company. Inhofe dumped his stock in PayPal, Apple, and a real estate company. Loeffler, whose husband is chairman of the New York Stock Exchange, made twenty-seven stock sales worth millions on the same day she attended a Senate briefing on the coronavirus. Seriously. Twenty-seven stock sales in one day. We can only assume she ignored her duties as an elected official—in a time of existential crisis—so she could take care of her personal finances.

Politicians are always quick to deny that they trade on insider information. Their investments are handled by a blind trust, they say. They don't learn about the trades until weeks later, if at all, they say. It's their spouse's account and their spouse's decision, they say. The Ethics Committee said it was okay, they say. But the timing and deftness of these trades cannot be denied. If you believe these politicians put your needs ahead of their own, you might as well also believe in Santa Claus. There's a bridge in Brooklyn I would like to sell you.

Burr's 2020 trades came on the heels of some other remarkable financial moves he's made. In 2018, for instance, he sold his shares in a Dutch fertilizer company when the shares were at an all-time high. The company had been set to benefit from US sanctions on Iranian oil and petrochemical imports. But when word started quietly circulating in Senate chambers that Trump was planning to waive those sanctions, Burr sold. The company's stocks plunged 40 percent a few weeks later when Trump's decision became public.

"How does he even know this Dutch company exists with all he has to do as chair of the Intelligence Committee and as a senior senator?" asked John Olson, a retired lawyer who helped draft insider trading legislation and often represents clients before the Securities and Exchange Commission. "How does he have time to research obscure companies in Holland?"

The only thing unusual about Burr's moves was the backlash. Elected officials make so many trades inspired by insider knowledge that hardly anyone pays attention anymore. But because of the uproar about his trades, Burr had to resign as chairman of the Senate Intelligence Committee. A few months later, he announced he wouldn't be running for reelection in 2022. Burr paid a price, but most politicians who cheat aren't penalized in any way. Yet he still used his office to become incredibly wealthy. So what did he lose by resigning? He lost the ability to continue to cheat and steal more money as an elected official.

Insider trading is just one of the tricks politicians use to get rich. They also buy real estate and then insert federal earmarks for public projects that enhance the worth of their property. They buy stock in companies while making laws that affect those firms. They pass legislation that benefits their investments and the industries that employ family members. They even sell their homes to lobbyists at inflated real estate values. And these shady politicians are not operating alone. They get help. As Mob boss Joe Bonanno once said, "It takes many stepping stones, you know, for a man to rise. None can do it unaided."

It's a racket. Make no mistake about it; if you or I tried to do some of this stuff, we'd go to jail. Of course, our elected leaders have created laws to make their illegal activities exempt from prosecution.

The Rich Get Richer

You don't get rich merely by getting elected to Congress. Lawmakers earn about $174,000 a year, and they aren't eligible for housing or per-diem allowances for expenses. They don't make extra for serving on committees. What's more, the high cost of living in the District of Columbia forces some lawmakers to share apartments or to bunk in someone's guest room. Some have been known to sleep in their offices.

As a result, some lawmakers struggle to make ends meet while in office. Rep. Steny Hoyer, a Democrat from Maryland, was the House majority leader in 2007, but between 2004 and 2010, his estimated wealth fell 90 percent. Between 2007 and the Great Recession of 2008, he lost about $250,000 in mutual funds. His colleague, Georgia Democrat Sanford Bishop, went from $184,000 in estimated wealth in 2004 to $159,000 in debt in 2010.

But Hoyer and Bishop are the exceptions rather than the rule. Most politicians, even those of modest means, grow rich in office, and the already-rich politicians just get richer and richer.

Between 2004 and 2012, the amount federal officeholders earned from outside jobs and investments nearly tripled, from $11.7 million to $31 million. According to the *Washington Post*, the median wealth of senators grew 73 percent from 2004 to 2010, from $1.5 million to $2.6 million. In the House, the median net worth of representatives has grown about 15 percent, from $650,000 in 2004 to $746,000 in 2010. The Center for Responsive Politics in Washington reported that members of Congress's net worth skyrocketed, on average, a jaw-dropping 84 percent between 2004 and 2006.

The subprime mortgage crisis and subsequent Great Recession from 2007 to 2010 decimated Americans' median net worth by 40 percent. In Congress? Well, a few people suffered. About twenty officeholders watched as their investment portfolios were cut in half.

But the rest of them flourished. Lawmakers' median wealth *rose* during the economic crisis, with some officeholders' portfolios growing nearly 15 percent.

How did they do that?

Profiting from Disaster

As the scope and severity of the subprime mortgage crisis became more and more apparent in Washington, many elected officials used their early insight to shore up their finances. Before the public discovered the devastating blow to their investments, many politicians had either protected themselves or capitalized on the crisis.

Rep. Spencer Bachus, the ranking Republican on the House Financial Services Committee, learned of the looming crisis through high-level meetings and weekend phone calls from Treasury Secretary Henry Paulson. From July 2008 to November of that year—the period in which the crisis went from whispered warnings to deafening alarm bells and a freefalling international economy—Bachus made no fewer than forty trades, actually betting on and profiting from the collapse of our economy.

According to Peter Schweizer in his book *Throw Them All Out*, Bachus made tens of thousands of dollars during this time by trading options. Options allow a trader to bet on a stock rising or falling, and Bachus's insider knowledge allowed him to bet heavily that stocks would fall. Bachus made dozens of these wagers, putting him in a position to profit while his unknowing constituents suffered staggering losses. Bachus, entrusted by the voters to lead us through a crisis like this, put himself in a position where it was to his advantage for the rest of us to get hammered. In other words, his HYPOCRISY caused his constituents, who elected him and trusted him, to lose while he gained dramatically.   2008

At one closed-door meeting in September, Bachus listened as Paulson and Federal Reserve Bank Chairman Ben Bernanke predicted a global financial free-fall. Lehman Brothers had already gone under, and General Motors was close to bankruptcy. Fannie Mae and Freddie Mac were on the lip of the abyss. Stocks would plummet, and no one was sure where the basement was.

The next day, Bachus bought options for $7,846. A few days later, after the market had fallen, he sold the options for $13,000. Bachus continued this practice, repeatedly betting that the market would fall and profiting when it did. He bought options on broad market funds but also options on specific companies. When General Electric officials notified Paulson that they were having trouble selling their bonds, Bachus bought GE call options, doubling his money on several different trades.

Bachus's practice of placing bets on falling stock prices was old hat. He'd been doing that for years. In 2007, for instance, he doubled his federal salary by buying options, often on companies like United Airlines and Microsoft that had business before one of his committees. Despite Schweizer's book and a related *60 Minutes* segment on the insider trading, Bachus was cleared in 2012 by the Office of Congressional Ethics, which claimed it had found no evidence of violations by the senator. Bachus retired in 2015.

It's no surprise that the Office of Congressional Ethics found no wrongdoing. They never do. They're toothless, slow, and secretive. In fact, you could say they are part of the corruption, and this, too, is just like the Mafia.

As crime boss Joe Bonanno once noted, "Mafia is a process, not a thing. Mafia is a form of clan—cooperation to which its individual members pledge lifelong loyalty. Friendship, connections, family ties, trust, loyalty, obedience—this was the glue that held us together." Is Congress's ridiculously spineless ethics enforcers the same kind of glue that encourages politicians to break the rules?

Get My Broker on the Phone

Bachus was not alone. House Minority Leader John Boehner met several times with Paulson for secret talks about the mortgage industry collapse, and within hours of one breakfast meeting about a $150 billion bailout plan, Boehner moved his money out of higher-risk mutual funds, safely dodging losses when the stock market dropped.

When Bernanke and Paulson met with several officeholders early in the crisis, Paulson, in his memoir *On the Brink*, recalled how lawmakers were stunned. Stunned, sure. But also selfish and dishonorable.

- Rep. Jim Moran, a Democrat from Virginia, embarked the next day on his busiest stock-trading activity of the year, dumping stock in Goldman Sachs and dozens of other companies and avoiding huge personal financial loss.
- Sen. John Kerry raced back to his office to dump mutual funds related to the financial industry. A month later, he bought nearly a million dollars in bargain-priced shares of Citigroup and Bank of America just before the Treasury Department announced that both banks would be getting billions in bailout funds. Kerry found a way to make money at both ends of the crisis. Kerry also made money

off the passage of Obamacare in 2010. In 2009, he and his wife purchased shares of a medical device manufacturer. Although early versions of Obamacare included higher taxes on medical device companies, Kerry fought those taxes and helped get the fees down in the final version of the law. As a result, shares in his device company rose 71 percent when Obamacare passed. Kerry's stock in hospital supplier Thermo Fisher Scientific rose 40 percent after Obamacare passed.

- West Virginia Republican Shelley Capito dumped up to $250,000 in stock in Citigroup the day after the Paulson–Bernanke meeting.
- Dick Durbin, the Democrat chairing the Subcommittee on Financial Services and General Government, sold $73,715 in stock, preventing a catastrophic loss when the stock market dropped 9 percent in early October and then another 22 percent two weeks later.

This kind of behavior was widespread. In 2008, members of the House alone had as much as $75 million invested in financial institutions. About one in three House members invested in financial institutions. The Senate's investment was also high; according to the *Guardian* newspaper, thirty-seven senators owned up to $33 million in banks and other financial institutions. Should they have kept an arm's length from the financial institutions they regulate? Machiavelli would have told them not to worry about it. "A wise ruler ought never to keep faith when by doing so it would be against his interests," Machiavelli once said.

And trading on inside information was not the full extent of the problem. One study at the University of Pennsylvania and the University of Chicago revealed that during the subprime mortgage bailout crisis, politicians' votes on bailout measures often aligned with their own stock investments. Politicians with investments in the financial sector were more likely to support bailouts for firms in that sector. Politicians who received campaign contributions from financial institutions were more likely to support their bailout. And there are signs that these public representatives continued to support these rich financiers long after the recession ended; one study found that politically connected hedge funds perform dramatically better than their counterparts who don't lobby or contribute to campaigns. Getting Rich on Insider Information.

How bad is this epidemic of graft and insider trading?

In 2004 and 2011, a small group of researchers used the financial disclosure reports of politicians to build model portfolios for our elected leaders. Then they charted the fabulous returns our officeholders routinely enjoy.

The researchers found that House members "earn statistically significant positive abnormal returns." They outperform the overall stock market by 6 percentage points. Senators, the study found, do even better. They beat the market by an unheard-of 10 percentage points a year. These people make Warren Buffett look like an amateur. Senate portfolios "show some of the highest excess returns ever recorded over a long period of time, significantly outperforming even hedge fund managers," with gains that are "both economically large and statistically significant," the study found.

Researcher Alan J. Ziobrowski, an associate professor at Georgia State University, said the lawmakers' stock profits are "beyond the area that we would call good fortune." The money lawmakers make on their stock trades is so significant, Ziobrowski said, that it's "not rational to assume that they are just plain dumb-lucky."

Cracking Down on Conflicts of Interest

When politicians are accused of putting their own financial interests ahead of their constituents, many of the accused call for a "full investigation" by a Congressional ethics panel. They have nothing to hide, and they want full transparency. This is what Burr did after he used insider information about COVID-19 to make stock trades.

But what the public often doesn't realize is that these ethics panels are a sham. The panels are stacked by the accused politician's peers, and they rarely discipline anyone. From 2012 to 2014, the Senate ethics panel dismissed every case that came before it. Why? We don't know why. The committee doesn't comment on cases or release details of its investigations.

What the Senate ethics panel *does* do is sanction their colleagues' questionable behavior. According to the *Washington Post*, members of Congress contact the House and Senate ethics offices thousands of times a year about potential conflicts of interest. From 2007 to 2011, for example, the offices issued 2,800 opinions, sent 6,500 emails, and took 40,000 phone calls, usually from lawmakers trying to justify their questionable financial maneuvers. Most of the time, the ethics folks rubberstamp the file with a festive "You're Good to Go!" This allows your elected leader to reassure the public that he is honest because he got approval from the ethics panel. Of course, you can't independently check because ethics opinions are not subject to public records laws.

Legislators don't have to identify potential conflicts when their official actions help their investments. Congress has required top executive branch officials to divest themselves of assets that pose a conflict of interest, but lawmakers have not required the same thing for themselves. They can freely invest in firms even as they create laws that can affect the profits of those firms. From 2007 to 2010, for instance, 131 elected officials (or close family members of those officials) bought and sold as much as $218 million in more than three hundred companies registered to lobby on issues coming before those same lawmakers. A *Washington Post* investigation found that seventy-three lawmakers sponsored bills that directly benefited their own or their families' business or industry.

That's why a California congressman was able to secure tax breaks for racehorse owners—and then go out and buy seven horses when the new rules took effect. If he'd been Italian, he would have easily fit in with Cosa Nostra. The Mob likes sure things—scams guaranteed to make money—and politicians know how to eliminate financial risks.

That's why a Wyoming congresswoman could sponsor legislation to double the length of grazing permits—which allowed her husband to make money while overgrazing public land owned by you and me. With gall like that, she could have been the first woman to become a made man and take the blood oath of omerta. Well, maybe she would be second only to Nancy Pelosi.

That's why a Pennsylvania congressman could get a natural gas bill passed—even though it helped his wife make millions selling shares in natural gas companies to ExxonMobil.

This is not how it's supposed to work. These are Mafia tactics.

"If you have major responsibility for drafting legislation that directly affects particular companies, then you shouldn't be trading in their stock," said Dennis Thompson, a professor of public policy at Harvard University's John F. Kennedy School of Government and author of *Ethics in Congress: From Individual to Institutional Corruption*.

A Dirty Cleanup

After a *60 Minutes* investigation revealed how politicians routinely use insider information, Congress passed the STOCK Act. STOCK stands for Stop Trading on Congressional Knowledge. The bill was about as substantial as wet toilet paper. It did not force lawmakers to stop trading stocks or to put their portfolios in a blind trust. It did not force them to stop passing bills that helped their companies or the industries they held stock in. It merely banned lawmakers from using inside knowledge to make trades. But, as Burr, Feinstein, Durbin, and others demonstrated, the practice continued.

The 2012 STOCK Act outlawed insider trading by members of Congress and their staffs, banned them from participating in IPOs, and required them to file detailed financial disclosures. The new rules also applied to other federal employees, including the president, vice president, and certain other members of the executive branch. Obama signed this bill to great fanfare. Congress was *not* above the law!

Within a year, Congress quietly passed an amendment to weaken the law's financial disclosure statements. No fanfare this time. No public signing ceremony by Obama. Under the revised law, top federal employees, including staffers on Capitol Hill and in the White House, no longer had to publicly disclose their financial holdings online. The requirement still applies to elected leaders and candidates, but even for them, the law is full of loopholes and opportunities to hide the true amount of the transactions. It was back to business as usual.

"On closer examination, it appears that what Congress really wants is to keep making the big bucks that come from trading on inside information but to trick those outside of the Beltway into believing they are doing something about this corruption," wrote Yale Law School scholar Jonathan Macey.

The slow rollback of the STOCK Act was no surprise to people like me who had been in the Mafia and had read *The Prince* by Machiavelli. "Never attempt to win by force what can be won by deception," the philosopher wrote. "Men are so simple of mind, and so much dominated by their immediate needs, that a deceitful man will always find plenty who are ready to be deceived."

How to Correct the Problem

What are the answers?

For starters, we can start electing officials who understand when something is unethical.

I'm never a big fan of government overregulation, but clearly these mobsters in Congress need stronger rules about handling their financial affairs while in office. Why don't we require Congress to put their investments in a blind trust, the way most presidents do? Why don't we set up more ethical boundaries?

One thing I like is the independent Office of Congressional Ethics, which is a nonpartisan watchdog set up in 2008 when lawmakers got tired of the slow-moving, toothless House Ethics Committee. The OCE has a staff of ten, and unlike the ethics committee, they actually investigate things. They accept anonymous complaints, and they pressure lawmakers to compel their staffers to answer questions. The OCE also makes its findings public.

The problem with the OCE is that it doesn't have much authority. It can't subpoena anyone, and it can't punish anyone. All it can do is forward its findings to the lawmakers' own ethics panel, which as we showed earlier in this chapter, never does anything with the information.

As a result, shady lawmakers who get investigated by the

OCE simply refuse to cooperate. That's what Rep. Rashida Tlaib, the Democrat from Michigan, did when the OCE asked why the congresswoman paid herself a salary from her campaign account. So did a Virginia Republican who would send his staff out to do his shopping and walk his dog, and Rep. Mark Meadows, who continued paying his chief of staff after barring him from the office for sexually harassing female staffers. Lawmakers simply refuse to cooperate, and there are no repercussions. In the first eight years of the OCE, 74 percent of lawmakers investigated cooperated with the office. Since 2016, that number has plummeted to 33 percent.

Again, elected officials think they should be above the law.

Chapter 5

The Price of Government Intrusion

"We cannot solve our problems with the same thinking we used when we created them."

—ALBERT EINSTEIN.

WHEN I FIRST PLANNED TO FRANCHISE MY IDEA FOR A new kind of pizza store, I figured it was a can't-miss proposition.

The restaurant is called Slices and my partner and friend, Tony Riviera, and I use only the absolute best ingredients. We visited several cities in Italy to sample the finest products, and we traveled to Spain and France to study the best bread-making techniques. We use red spring flour from Naples for our pies, and we let the dough ferment to cut down on yeast. Our tomatoes come from Campania and our olive oil from Sicily. Even our special pans and ovens come from Italy. We set it up so that all these ingredients come together easily, so the store could be run by only three or four people, making it more profitable.

What we didn't anticipate was how difficult it would be to

meet all the rules and regulations for opening a restaurant in California. We needed permits for everything, inspections for this and that, and mountains of paperwork for federal Small Business Administration loans. We had to follow rules about hiring, hours, lighting, signage, and employee benefits. We needed sign permits, employee health permits, resale permits, building health permits, seller's permits. We needed a business license, a food service license, a liquor license, and a music license. Certificates of occupancy. There seemed to be no end to the red tape.

This is the kind of government interference small business owners face every day. In fact, if you ask most small business owners, they'll complain more about red tape than they do about their taxes. A 2017 survey by the Kauffman Foundation found that businesses feel more overregulated than overtaxed; two-thirds say they pay a "fair share" of taxes but are overwhelmed by complicated and overlapping federal, state, and local rules about hiring, zoning, permits, health insurance, training, and other aspects of starting or expanding a business. Entrepreneurs in the survey gave California an "F" grade for ease of doing business, but they also felt unwelcome in several states in the Northeast. The United States is supposed to be the land of free enterprise, a place where smart, hardworking businesses can get started and flourish. Overregulation is destroying that idea.

And it's not just restaurants that struggle. The Competitive Enterprise Institute, a conservative think tank, estimates that the cost of complying with America's federal regulations was $1.86 trillion in 2013—about $15,000 per household. Some of those regulations yield benefits, from clean air to toasters that don't catch fire, but most of our regulations are passed without any consideration for how they will affect people. A 2010 study for the Small Business Administration, a government body, found that regulations in general add $10,585 in costs per employee.

Should our government be working so hard to hold people and businesses back this way? What's with all these regulations?

This overregulation is another example of how the government acts like the Mob.

The Mafia's power came from its ability to exert control over people, their businesses, or their property. We wanted to control almost every aspect of people's lives, from the house they built, to the food that they ate, to the clothes they wore, to the music they listened to. And if you made a bet on a horse or a sporting event, you were doing it with a Mob bookie.

The more control we exerted over people's lives, the wealthier our Mafia families became. The hierarchy of the Mafia employs the same philosophy within the organization. Every made man having the rank of soldier is required to place all of their business dealings "on record" with their caporegime. In other words, the bosses need to know where a soldier's income is coming from and, quite often, how much he is earning.

Similarly, every soldier requires their associates to put all their business dealings on record with them. The bosses say this policy was designed to protect the soldier from marauding wiseguys who might try to lay a claim to their business and grab part of their money. While that might be true, the real reason is control! The bosses want to know what their underlings are earning so they get a piece of the action. If a soldier messes up, violates Mob policy in any way, he might stand to lose his entire business to his boss. The Mafia's formula: power + control = wealth.

Our government follows the same formula.

Strangled in Red Tape

And it's only getting worse. According to the Committee for Economic Development, the number of people employed at federal regulatory agencies has grown from fifty thousand in 1960 to nearly three hundred thousand today. Total spending for creating and enforcing federal regulations grew from nothing sixty years ago to more than $70 billion in 2016. Between 1970 and 2008, the number of prescriptive words like "shall" or "must" in the code of federal regulations grew from 403,000 to nearly 963,000. That's about 15,000 new edicts a year—a rate that Obama accelerated during his two terms. Obama got rule-generating behemoth laws like the Affordable Care Act and the Dodd–Frank bill passed, but when Congress stopped cooperating with his regulation jamboree, Obama just kept issuing new ones through executive fiat.

Dodd–Frank is a great example of how complicated our government has become. When the stock market crashed in 1929, Congress passed the forty-page Glass–Steagall Act to place limitations on banks' risky investments. In 2010, after the banks' risky behavior with subprime loans brought us to the brink of a second Great Depression, Congress passed the 850-page Dodd–Frank bill to rein the banks back in.

Dodd–Frank is a monument to government overregulation. Even at almost a thousand pages, it was still mostly an outline for more regulations. One rule outlined in the law includes 383 questions that break down into 1,420 subquestions. It calls for more than four hundred different rules, many of which haven't even been written yet by federal regulatory agencies. It's a law that just continues to spawn more and more regulations. Outspoken musician Terre Thaemlitz hit the nail on the head when he declared that "laws never protect anyone, despite claiming to be all about protecting the public. Each legal restriction only strengthens the power of Mafia and crime (organizations) who step in to help people do what the law says they can't do, in every country.

Don't get me wrong. I'm not in favor of a lawless society, not by any means. Even when I was a mobster, I was not in favor of lawlessness. If you don't have law and order, people like mobsters who are willing to break the rules would have no advantage over people who follow the rules.

This is one reason why politicians and lawmakers are so effective at lining their own pockets; they can break the rules that hold others back. In fact, politicians have a distinct advantage over mobsters because they have the power to write rules that exempt them from restrictions that hold everyone else in check. Former Mob boss Paul Castellano said it well. "This life of ours, this is a wonderful life," Castellano said one time. "If you can get through life like this and get away with it, hey, that's great. But it's very, very unpredictable. There's so many ways you can screw it up." If you're a politician, it's much more predictable. You can cheat without risk.

But overregulation is having dramatic effects on our country. It's slowing down economic growth and entrepreneurial innovation. It's widening the gap between the rich and poor. It's killing jobs and cutting pay. One study I read found that a 10 percent increase in state regulations increases prices by 1 percent and a 10 percent increase in state regulations increases poverty by 25 percent. Federal regulations have increased by 30 percent in the last fifteen years.

Most of these regulations and their costs are hidden from view. According to the World Bank's chief economist, Kaushik Basu, the effects are too deep for us to see. The impact is on the guy who has to stay up late filling out paperwork for imports or exports. It's the entrepreneur who wastes a year trying to get a license before abandoning his plan to open a new business. It's the executive of a hot new startup who looks at the rules for an initial public offering and says, "The hell with that. Let's stay private."

They may be hidden, these sad events, but they are happening. After the Enron fraud, Congress passed the Sarbanes–Oxley law to prevent future scams by hugely profitable corporations cooking the books. But that law, like Dodd–Frank, had many unintended consequences. Sarbox made it so difficult to list shares on an American stock exchange that the United States' share of initial public offerings plummeted from 67 percent in 2002 to 16 percent a decade later. The rest of the world was innovating and letting investors in on great ideas so they could flourish, while the US seemed to have run out of ideas.

We all pay the price of trying to comply with a complex government. For instance, many Americans have to hire a professional to prepare their taxes every year. In Britain, you don't have to hire anyone, and many people don't even have to file. According to the IRS Taxpayer Advocate Service, Americans spend more than 6 billion hours each year complying with the tax code, and the direct and indirect costs of it amount to $163 billion. According to the National Commission on Fiscal Responsibility and Reform, if we simplified the tax code—leaving just deductions for the earned income tax credit, the child tax credit, and a few others—marginal rates on middle-income taxpayers would be cut in half. Top earner rates would be cut by a third. And the government would not see a drop in revenue.

Simplify.

Look at social security, a simple, old-school law. Those benefits are readily available, and when you start taking yours at sixty-two, sixty-seven, or seventy, the check arrives each month with the taxes already taken out. Compare that with a 401(k),

IRAs, and 529 accounts. Those are the new-school systems, and the rules, penalties, investment choices, and withdrawal demands take time, research, and careful evaluation to understand. It's tricky, with a lot of time-sensitive decisions to make. It's so complicated that a lot of people just don't bother. No wonder most Americans are so woefully unprepared for retirement; according to the Economic Policy Institute, the median retirement account balance among those between the ages of fifty-six and sixty-one is a measly $21,000.

Our understanding of health insurance might be even worse than our grasp on retirement accounts. One recent study found that only 14 percent of those with health insurance understand what deductibles and co-pays are.

Listen, it's not just average citizens who get mired in this thick soup. As a country, we struggle to repair and expand our basic infrastructure because of all the rules and regulations our country has put on the process. When they wanted to upgrade the Bayonne Bridge between Staten Island and New Jersey and elevate the road so big cargo ships could pass, the job required forty-seven permits from nineteen different government entities. Contractors had to do a historical survey of every building within two miles of the bridge, even those not affected by the project in any way. The regulatory process alone took four years.

This was not a rare incident. The problem is so bad that both Obama and Trump had trouble identifying "shovel-ready" public works projects to fund with stimulus money. According to one study, big highway projects approved in 2015 took on average a decade to clear every bureaucratic hurdle.

Other Damaging Developments

Before we talk about who's to blame for this overregulation and what we can do about it, we need to acknowledge just how dangerous this complex web of regulation is. The booming growth of federal regulation is being matched by corresponding local and state regulations, creating an even more complex web that holds our heads underwater.

When Hurricane Katrina struck New Orleans, for instance, neither the federal government nor the state government was certain who was in charge of the city's levee system. Seriously. No one knew. A 2007 study found that the "tangled joint administration" of the city's flood-protection system played a key role in the devastation of the city. Can you believe that? Look at the lives that were devastated as a result of government regulation, interference, and ineptness.

"Because administering programs through intergovernmental cooperation introduces pervasive coordination problems into even rather simple governmental functions, the odds are high that programs involving shared responsibility will suffer from sluggish administration, blame-shifting, and unintended consequences," noted political scientist Steven Teles of Johns Hopkins, who has coined the term *kludgeocracy* to describe our overly complex, highly regulated government.

Teles says the term *kludge* comes from computer programming and describes it as an "inelegant patch" that fixes an unexpected problem. Our government's rules and regulations are kludges taped to our laws and agencies. The problems occur when you apply an inordinate number of these patches to create a complex system that has no unifying goal or intent. "When you add up enough kludges, you get a very complicated program that has no clear organizing principle, is exceedingly difficult to understand, and is subject to crashes. Any user of Microsoft Windows will immediately grasp the concept," Teles wrote in *National Affairs*.

Are the Rules Effective? Who Knows?

The real problem for political scientists like Teles is that these kludges are applied to our regulatory system with scant attention paid to their overall impact. No one really knows if most of these rules and regulations do what they were intended to do, and very few are reviewed after the fact to see if they are working. That's why fifty-year-old FAA regulations aimed at preventing sonic booms continue to hamstring startups trying to build lighter, quieter, and commercially viable supersonic jets.

Lawmakers only glance at the effect of the regulations they pass. Every president for the last forty years has ordered federal agencies to analyze their rules to ensure they are solving problems in a cost-efficient manner. Dutifully, each year, the Office of Information and Regulatory Affairs issues an annual report to Congress on the benefits and costs of regulations. That all sounds good, but the reviews are, at best, superficial.

Here's why: Since 1980, the relatively tiny OIRA office has been cut in half, to just forty-five people. Meanwhile, the number of regulations has increased exponentially. While OIRA has been shrinking, the number of agency regulators—the people who are writing the rules—has doubled to 292,000 people. Think about that for a second. For each person responsible for evaluating the effectiveness of rules and regulations, there are nearly 6,500 people writing new rules.

According to researchers Jerry Ellig and Richard Williams at the Regulatory Studies Center at George Washington University, the number of new regulations that are analyzed for costs and benefits before passage amounts to a tiny fraction of the total number of new regulations that are approved. From 2008 to 2013, for instance, 14,795 federal regulations were introduced. About 10 percent of these were considered significant enough to justify an OIRA review. About 2 percent were so significant that a review was *required by law*. But only eighty-two—0.6 percent of the total—were reviewed for economic benefits and costs. Our regulatory oversight system is a net with holes big enough for a whale to swim through.

"As a result," Ellig and Williams wrote, "neither the president nor Congress nor the public has any knowledge of whether the billions (if not trillions) of dollars of expenditures to produce and comply with regulations are improving outcomes for the American people."

When it comes to weeding out anachronistic or ineffective rules, the US is way behind the times. According to the Organisation for Economic Cooperation and Development, a sixty-year-old international group of thirty-seven of the world's richest democratic-capitalist countries, fifteen countries do a better job of this than we do. Australia is the best. It has an independent agency devoted to unearthing old rules that no longer work or whose cost doesn't justify the reward.

To his credit, Obama tried to improve our efforts to do this when he ordered federal agencies to ferret out archaic rules. It worked for a while. The Department of Transportation, for instance, eliminated a rule that truck drivers must file a vehicle condition report before and after every trip, even when there was nothing to report. The trucking industry rejoiced. Getting rid of that rule saved them about $1.7 billion. By some accounts, Obama issued 101 rules that reduced compliance costs for US businesses, saving them nearly $8 billion annually and freeing the equivalent of sixty-two thousand employees working full time on paperwork. All told, Obama took eighteen major actions on deregulation. But all those gains were obliterated by new rules. In 2016 alone, Obama burdened US business with 118 major new rules.

Which Party Is to Blame?

Democrats and Republicans both have to take responsibility for this mountain of red tape. Democrats like Obama and Clinton loved issuing new rules and regulations, but according to experts at George Washington University, Republican administrations often pass as many economically significant regulations as Democrats. One exception was Reagan, who approved far fewer regulations than other presidents. Bush 41 and Bush 43, however, each approved as many as Clinton.

The rules we're talking about here are major actions. They have an annual effect on the economy of more than $100 million, drastically increase costs or prices, or have a colossal impact on competition, employment, investment, productivity, and innovation. Overall, Democratic presidents annually average seventy-nine major rules, and Republicans average sixty-two. Trump was way below both averages during his first two years in office, but he made up for lost time in the third when he published eighty-seven major rules.

But no one comes close to Obama. This guy loved rules and regulations, and the major bills passed under his watch generated an ungodly horde of costly new regulations.

Obamacare tried to reduce the number of people without medical insurance, but it did so by unleashing a staggering volume of new rules and regulations. Congressional staff don't have the time or the expertise to write these rules, so lawmakers turned the job over to those 290,000 regulatory folks they have on staff. Bureaucrats cranked out thousands of pages of new rules. The result is that the number of categories for illness and injury alone rose from 18,000 to over 140,000. And some of these new treatment codes are ridiculous. There are nine codes for injuries caused by parrots and three related to burns caused by flaming water skis. Believe this? How many of you reading this have been injured by a parrot or burned by a flaming water ski? What the heck is a flaming water ski? I water-ski. Never saw one go up in flames. Seriously. What's not comical is how healthcare providers now have to spend an hour doing government paperwork for every hour they spend treating patients.

I'm not making this stuff up.

Once he figured out that the Republicans weren't going to rubber-stamp his legislative moves, Obama turned to presidential fiat to continue churning out the regulations. He issued new regulations under the Clean Air Act and the Clean Water Act. He expanded mandatory overtime pay for workers on low salaries. He banned telecom firms from favoring one type of internet traffic. He issued new rules for investment advisors.

Obama's lust for executive orders alarmed a lot of people. Never mind the so-called "deep state." Conservatives described Obama's rulemaking penchant as the new "administrative state."

This had Republicans pulling out their hair. Regulations are a major drag on economic growth, and deregulation has become almost as important to Republicans as tax cuts.

Trump did what he could to undo Obama's handiwork. Trump signed an executive order requiring that for every new rule that increases regulatory costs, at least two old ones have to be eliminated to reduce regulatory costs by the same amount. Britain started doing that in 2011 and found so many half-witted regulations that they increased the ratio from "one in, one out" to "one in, three out."

The big reason Republicans push deregulation is because businesses—particularly small businesses—plead for relief. Costly new government regulations often force businesses to fire employees or to put off expansion. When Congress raises the minimum wage, for instance, teenage employment typically drops off. Doesn't that make sense? if a business can't afford to hire an employee at a government-mandated minimum wage, THEY DON'T HIRE. How does this help either a business or a potential worker? A company should be allowed to set its own wages with a REASONABLE minimum wage in place. When Congress passed the Family and Medical Leave Act in 1993, a study found that firms with 60 employees would be more profitable if they cut back to 49 employees. When the Americans with Disabilities Act was passed, it actually convinced many businesses to remain small enough to avoid the costly regulations.

Conservatives and business people particularly hate it when Congress mandates worker benefits like retirement, workers' comp, unemployment insurance, and the like. According to the conservative think tank the Heritage Foundation, these kinds of regulations can actually *decrease* an employee's overall compensation while *increasing* an employer's expense. In other words, no one wins.

"One way or another, much of the cost of the regulation will end up being borne by the workers, whether in the form of fewer jobs, fewer fringe benefits, a reduction in the growth of wages over time, or some combination of the three," wrote economist William Laffer.

Environmental laws can be particularly damaging. By 1990, laws like the Clean Air Act and the Endangered Species Act reduced employment by more than 1 percent—over a million jobs. What's more, the high cost of labor has driven many companies to other countries and damaged US competitiveness with foreign business. When you're living under the constant threat of new regulations, many business owners are unlikely to expand, hire, or invest until the future is more certain.

How Corporations Make Things Worse

Our lawmakers' passion for overregulation can be partly explained as hubris. Congress and the rule-writers spool out enormous laws like Dodd–Frank with the goal of closing every possible loophole. They want to think they can lay down rules that cover every possibility. But the complexity only opens the door to new loopholes, more uncertainty, and the opportunity for special interests to sneak in and secure favorable treatment that their competitors don't enjoy.

When new rules are proposed, the lobbyists for Wall Street, banks, healthcare, mining, oil, aviation, and other giant industries use their influence in Washington to carve out exemptions for themselves. The politicians, who are collecting campaign contributions and investing their own money in these firms, are only happy to oblige. The result is regulations that are even more complex and whose overall value is harder to measure. As the British magazine the *Economist* puts it, "The government's drive to micromanage so many activities creates a huge incentive for interest groups to push for special favours. When a bill is hundreds of pages long, it is not hard for congressmen to slip in clauses that benefit their chums and campaign donors."

Economists call this activity "rent-seeking," which we talked about in Chapter 2. Corporations have learned that it's worth the investment to hire lobbyists to finagle these hidden deals. In fact, they've also learned that complex rules and regulations can have the added benefit of discouraging competitors from entering the market. Corporations that lobby get the best of both worlds: Not only do they gain exemptions to rules that apply to everyone else, but they can keep future competitors from challenging their profits. They can raise prices without worrying about losing customers. It's a beautiful scam. It's called "crony capitalism." Businesses thrive not as a result of taking risks or pursuing innovation but through a mutually beneficial relationship with the rule-makers. It's not free-market capitalism at all.

And it has a serious downside, not the least of which is unfair and overly complex regulations. Another impact is that it discourages economic growth. When brilliant entrepreneurs develop a market-altering idea, they can't get their innovation onto the market.

This is a travesty. It hurts our economy, and it hurts our competitiveness in the global economy. Our economy is not growing. Our personal income has been stagnant for twelve years. Our children make less than we do and don't expect the situation to improve. We lose faith that our government can ever be an effective tool for the good of society as a whole.

Our complex web of rules and regulations has the plain impact of making sure everyone is obedient to the government. Philosopher and linguist Noam Chomsky saw this happening on a global scale. "International affairs is very much run like the mafia," Chomsky noted. "The godfather does not accept disobedience, even from a small storekeeper who doesn't pay his protection money. You have to have obedience, otherwise the idea can spread that you don't have to listen to the orders and it can spread to important places."

Something's got to give. But what?

I have a few ideas.

Solutions

Listen, I'm a conservative, but I'm not in favor of the wholesale lifting of government regulations the way some Republicans are.

We used to believe that financial markets have the ability to "self-regulate," but the housing collapse and the Great Recession exploded that myth. We lost eight million jobs, and millions of families lost their homes. Trillions of dollars in wealth disappeared. That's what voluntary regulation got us. Dodd–Frank was a nightmare of regulations, but banks are more solvent as a result, and the ridiculous salaries paid in the financial industry have been slashed. The financial industry, with all its deceitful practices and worthless products, has been rightfully trimmed way back.

And who is going to argue against something like the Food Safety Modernization Act of 2010? That law gave the Food and Drug Administration increased power to mandate product recalls—something we used to leave up to the industry—and even the food industry supported it because it bolstered consumer confidence, and that's good for business. Not all regulations are bad.

There are plenty of other examples of regulations whose benefits far outweigh their cost. The Clean Air Act amendments of 1990 saved more than 160,000 lives, and the economic benefits exceeded $1.3 trillion—twenty-five times as much as it costs to comply with its regulations.

The problem is not with these laws but with the narrow, overly detailed regulations that are taped over with so many special-interest exemptions that you can't recognize the original intent of the law. These result from overzealous rule-writers and lobbyists and also from the circuitous route many of these regulations take on their way to becoming law. Some bills like Dodd–Frank go through committee after committee, and at each step, lawmakers have an opportunity to tack on a favor for a friend or funder. It's ridiculous. It should be criminal because it benefits the lawmaker and the special interests and not the people. So are the Senate filibuster rules that allow lawmakers to demand changes to a bill in exchange for their vote.

We need to simplify.

- We need to do a better job analyzing rules and regulations to ensure they do what they were intended to do. We need to review old rules and see if they are working. We need an independent watchdog agency with the resources to systematically cull outdated regulations that cost more than we get back or that stifle economic growth. Every rule should have a sunset clause so that it expires unless Congress formally reauthorizes it.
- We need simpler rules that lay down broad goals and prescribe only what is strictly required to achieve them. We need to end this practice of passing sprawling omnibus bills that have no clear purpose other than to allow every single Congressman to tack on their pet project, earmark, or special-interest exemption.
- The federal government needs to quit delegating so much to the states and making it difficult to determine who is responsible for what. I like George Mason scholar Michael Greve's notion of "one problem, one sovereign."
- The feds should also follow the model set by several states that are actively working to reduce their stranglehold on their people and economies. Kentucky, for instance, has a red-tape reduction initiative that has reduced the state's administrative regulations by nearly 30 percent. Rhode Island, Virginia, and Idaho are also reevaluating their regulatory codes.
- We need to continue the work Trump started by reforming occupational licensing requirements. Too many jobs require licenses. Florists, casket makers, cosmetologists, and tour guides are among the hundreds of jobs that require licenses. It's ridiculous. Some of these licenses cost thousands of dol-

lars and months of costly classes. The time and money spent to get a license discourages many low-income workers from getting better jobs, and studies have shown that licensing only serves to increase prices while doing little to improve the quality of the work. In their book *Captured Economy*, Steven Teles and Brink Lindsay found that 30 percent of all American jobs now require a license—up from 5 percent in the 1950s—and the purpose is often to restrict competition for incumbent businesses. This hurts us all, but it particularly hurts the poor. And the poor quite often are mostly comprised of minorities. Where are the cries of racism? I don't hear them.

- It's not just licensing that's holding back vast swaths of our population from getting better jobs and more income. In many cities, government restrictions on building drive up the cost of housing for the poor and lower middle class. As a result, these people can't find housing they can afford that's close to the jobs they need. Many of the zoning restrictions that create this problem only serve to protect the interests of existing property owners and developers, further widening the gap between rich and poor. According to one report from the Brookings Institute, our country's gross domestic product might be nearly 10 percent higher if workers had access to all these jobs from which they are currently cut off.

- We need a name for these overregulation problems so people can identify them and complain about them. I like Teles's term "kludgeocracy." It suggests the blunt-force, heavy-handed wastefulness of our current system. Ordinary citizens like you and I need to be able to see these problems for the impenetrable web they have become. Most people are ignorant of what's going on because it's all hidden or obscured by...*overregulation*. When we are struggling to fill out a federal education loan form or determine how much of our travel expenses should be deducted or whether we need a county permit or a city permit or a state permit, we need to email our elected representatives and insist they work toward ending this insidious process that is doing so much damage to our economy and private lives.

- Conservatives need to broaden their perspective. They always evaluate regulations in terms of how it affects jobs. They have a one-track argument, and it's too limited. Environmental regulations may eliminate certain jobs, but maybe we don't want those jobs. Clean air and water save lives, improve health, lower healthcare costs, and ensure healthier, more productive workers, and you have to admit that is good for business.

- We need to be clear about who benefits from regulations. When Uber and Lyft arrived on the scene, they were hailed as the perfect capitalist response to an emerging situation: riders who wanted fast, convenient service in areas where cabs weren't plentiful or readily available. But then we started hearing people calling for more costly regulation of the ridesharing operators. These drivers needed to be vetted to protect the consumer! We needed fingerprint checks! We needed fare meters and seat checks! Was the flood of restrictions and new regulations for the benefit of consumers? Or did governments across the country clamp down to protect their entrenched (and often monopolistic) cab companies?

I understand there are no simple solutions and that changing the way our local and federal governments operate is not going to happen quickly. But maybe we can chip away at it.

Law professor Ilya Somin of George Mason University, the author of *Democracy and Political Ignorance: Why Smaller Gov-*

ernment is Smarter, points out that although our individual votes have only a small impact on these issues, we can have a big impact by voting with our feet. We can move from our overregulated cities and states to places that are working to simplify their government.

We can become foot voters.

"Foot voters know that their decisions matter and therefore work harder to seek out relevant information," Somin says. "Historically, even poorly educated and disadvantaged people have done a good job of identifying which jurisdictions offer the best opportunities and public services. If the essence of political freedom is making informed choices that make a real difference, foot voting fits the bill."

I agree.

Chapter 6

The Propaganda We Pay For

"Who controls the past controls the future. Who controls the present controls the past."

—GEORGE ORWELL

WHEN PRESIDENT OBAMA WAS CRAFTING THE AFFORD-able Care Act in 2009, his sweeping reforms frequently got a boost from a prominent MIT economist. His name was Jonathan Gruber, and he'd helped craft the healthcare bill in Massachusetts that became the model for Obamacare. As an independent expert, his support for Obamacare—and the factual background he provided—carried a lot of weight. People knew him and trusted him.

Reporters loved Gruber. He could explain complex economic principles in simple terms, and he often provided data the news media couldn't get elsewhere. Gruber promoted Obamacare in countless interviews and was a key source for stories in *Time* magazine, the *New York Times*, the *Atlantic* and the *New Republic.* Gruber also wrote his own essays touting the proposed law and even testified before two Senate committees responsible for healthcare legislation.

While always eager to endorse Obamacare, Gruber was not so eager to reveal one important fact: he wasn't the independent, unbiased source he'd let on to be. In reality, he was secretly making nearly half a million dollars as a "technical consultant" working on Obamacare for the federal Department of Health and Human Services. He failed to mention that fact to the reporters who quoted him, the politicians who listened to his testimony, and the editors who published his essays. The truth about Gruber's conflict of interest and subterfuge over Obamacare didn't come out until he wrote an editorial for the *New England Journal of Medicine.* The journal has a strict disclosure policy, and *NEJM* readers who took the time to review Gruber's disclosure forms learned he was actually being paid $400,000 by the Obama administration. Follow the money to expose the frauds.

This is the hypocrisy we need to deal with. It's "policy for sale." Obama needed someone credible to push his healthcare reform, so he found a candidate and PAID him to push it. Truth be damned and conflict of interest be damned.

Ostensibly he'd been hired to do calculations on the economic impact of Obamacare, but the truth was that Jonathan Gruber was a paid shill, a key cog in the propaganda machinery that led to the passage of Obamacare in 2010.

Gruber wasn't alone in misleading the public about Obamacare. Obama denied Gruber ever "worked on our staff" and the president never talked about how he and Gruber and the head of the Congressional Budget Office sat down together in the Oval Office to study the proposed measure. Nancy Pelosi said she didn't know Gruber, even though she had repeatedly cited him by name during the Obamacare debate. This is the type of two-faced behavior that today's politicians openly practice, and we the people chalk it all up as "politics as usual." But we should not stand for these lies. Would you accept constant lying from your spouse, partners, or friends? NO. Then why allow it from leaders you entrust and pay for to make decisions in your best interests? It's almost as if Obama had taken advice from crime boss Arnold Rothstein, who once said, "If a man is dumb, someone is going to get the best of him, so why not you? If you don't, you're as dumb as he is." You know how many times my caporegime said that to me when I was a Mob soldier? Even said it myself at times. Pure Mob thinking.

That was just the beginning of the duplicity surrounding Obamacare. The president repeatedly insisted that the individual mandate "is absolutely not a tax increase," even though Gruber—considered by many to be the architect of the legislation—admitted later that it was. He said the tax increase had to be written in a "tortured way" so the Congressional Budget Office wouldn't flag it as a tax, and he credited the "stupidity" of the American public for why voters didn't see it as a tax either. Yes, Obama and his hired gun called you "stupid" for buying into his lie that is Obamacare. As Machiavelli once said, "He who seeks to deceive will always find someone who will allow himself to be deceived." In the case of Obamacare, we allowed ourselves to be deceived.

"If you have a law that makes it explicit that healthy people pay in and sick people get money, it wouldn't have passed," Gruber said in one video. "Lack of transparency is a huge political advantage, and basically call it the stupidity of the American voter or whatever, but basically that was really critical to getting the thing to pass." Cosa Nostra members believe that anyone who is not a "made man" is a "sucker!" You can be a congressman, the president, or the pope, but you're still a "sucker," ripe for the taking. Obama and his cohorts apparently took us all for suckers and even went a step further in degrading us all by calling us all "stupid."

Again, Machiavelli hit the nail on the head. "Men are so simple and yield so readily to the desires of the moment that he who will trick will always find another who will suffer to be tricked."

The Gruber affair was not the first time our elected officials have misled the public with propaganda disguised as unbiased, factual information. In fact, it's pretty commonplace, although we don't hear much about it. In 2007, for instance, the Federal Emergency Management Agency hosted a phony press conference, with FEMA staffers posing as reporters. In 2004, the Bush administration hired a TV journalist to promote the No Child Left Behind bill while keeping it a secret that the journalist was on the payroll. In 2009, then–Vice President Joe Biden bragged that the Obama stimulus package had created or saved 650,000 jobs, citing data on a government website that investigators later found to be "fictitious and misleading."

How many times has Biden lied to us since becoming president? It's hard to keep track. His biggest whopper came when he claimed Georgia's controversial, Republican-backed election had shortened voting hours (it hadn't). He also repeatedly lied that federal contracts "awarded directly to foreign companies" rose by 30 percent under Trump. Again, not true. He lied about how many jobs his infrastructure plan would create, claiming 19 million jobs when only 2.7 million can be attributed to the plan itself. He also claimed he helped craft an $800 billion strategy to help Central America. Whoops! It was only $750 million.

Biden told several lies related to his pullout from Afghanistan:

- He vowed to provide the Afghan army with air support. He even promised Afghan President Ashraf Ghani he would, in a July 23 phone call. But by August 14, the US had pulled all its air support, intelligence, and contractors servicing Afghanistan's planes and helicopters, essentially putting the country's military on the sidelines as the Taliban stormed through the country and assumed power.
- When asked about intelligence reports that the Afghan government would quickly collapse after the US departure, Biden said, "That's not true...The likelihood there's going to be the Taliban overrunning everything and owning the whole country is highly unlikely." Highly unlikely. It took about five minutes for the Taliban to take over Afghanistan. Joe, were you blatantly lying, or did you not hear what your own intelligence experts were telling you? Either way, it raises questions about your fitness for office.
- Biden even tried to get Ghani to lie. The perception is "that things are not going well in the fight against the Taliban," Biden told Ghani. "And there is a need, whether it is true or not, there is a need to project a different picture." The soon-to-be-ousted Afghan president declined to embrace that fallacy. "We are facing a full-scale invasion, composed of Taliban, full Pakistani planning and logistical support, and at least ten thousand to fifteen thousand international terrorists, predominantly Pakistanis, thrown into this."

Biden stumbled badly in his first one hundred days. "The new ruler must determine all the injuries that he will need to inflict," Machiavelli once said. "He must inflict them once and for all."

Republican administrations have used your tax dollars to trick you, but few presidents took it to the same level as Obama.

Obama routinely used federal resources to promote his political agenda, using fraudulent and unproven "facts" to persuade voters and policymakers to go along with his plans. Most politicians utilize propaganda techniques to get elected, but Obama continued to deceive the public after he entered office. In 2009, when Obama had Democratic majorities in both the House and Senate, he was particularly brazen about it.

In a 2010 report, the House Oversight and Government Reform Committee acknowledged the president's right to promote his policies to the public and to Congress. But when the president uses federal resources to do the job, the committee said, it amounts to "an abuse of office and a betrayal of the president's pledge to create 'an unprecedented level of openness in government.'"

"The White House used the machinery of the Obama campaign to tout the President's agenda through inappropriate and sometimes unlawful public relations and propaganda initiatives," the committee found. "Many of the Obama administration's propaganda activities are unlawful because they are covert."

What happened to Obama? Nothing. Did he stop deceiving? No, because there are no consequences for the privileged in office.

Again, this is just one more example of Machiavelli in action in our government. In fact, when it comes to propaganda and deceit, Obama could have schooled both Machiavelli and more than a few mobsters on this tactic. "Princes and governments are far more dangerous than other elements within society," Machiavelli once wrote. "It is much more secure to be feared than to be loved."

Why Propaganda Is Wrong

When we think of propaganda, most of us think of totalitarian regimes. Propaganda hides inconvenient facts to create a rose-colored world. It distorts the truth in an effort to convince us to believe the way our policymakers want us to believe. It's a way for elected officials to *persuade* us with slanted declarations rather than to *inform* us with unclouded truth.

Democracy depends on the government communicating honestly with us. We can't hold our leaders accountable if we don't know the truth about their plans or activities. How will healthcare reform affect our insurance coverage? Are economic stimulus packages truly creating jobs and saving businesses? Is increasing the minimum wage good for our economy, or does it destroy jobs? Where will the hurricane make landfall? Does hydroxychloroquine cure COVID-19? As citizens, we have a right to clear, untainted answers to these and untold other questions.

But propaganda obscures the line between fact and fiction. It corrupts a basic premise of democracy—that our government exists to serve its citizens, not the other way around. If we can't trust the information we get from our government, we find ourselves living in a wary, cynical world where even fundamental truths are suspect. We can't govern ourselves when our elected government is manipulating us with false claims and misleading information. When you log into the Department of Labor website to check unemployment figures, you shouldn't be confronted with one-sided claims about how great a higher minimum wage would be for the economy. When you log into the Health and Human Services website to learn about Medicare, you shouldn't find pleas to lobby your congressional representative to support the president's healthcare overhaul. But that's exactly what we encountered during the Obama administration.

"We have a right to know which companies receive government contracts, how to collect insurance benefits and social security payments, and what public school educational reform will look like," says John Maxwell Hamilton, a scholar at the Woodrow Wilson Center for International Scholars. "But too often, the government uses its information machinery to do more than simply inform us about a policy. Sometimes, it tries to persuade us to adopt a particular position, regardless of its efficacy."

How We Got Here

In his book *Manipulating the Masses*, Hamilton traces the use of propaganda in the US to Woodrow Wilson, who created the Committee on Public Information to promote the country's entry into World War I. The office, headed up by a muckraker named Howard Creel, soon had offices around the world and was churning out press releases, films, commercials, ads, and cartoons. Creel had one goal in mind: "America must be thrilled into unity and projectile force" in its effort to end the Great War raging in Europe. As many as seventy-five thousand orators were recruited to give patriotic speeches during movie theater intermissions, and dissent towards Wilson's goal of "making the world safe for democracy" was quashed. In its eighteen-month existence, the CPI "shot propaganda through every capillary of the American bloodstream," Hamilton wrote.

The federal government would continue to use propaganda during times of war. Franklin Roosevelt held "fireside chats" that were scripted by his policy advisers. The Works Progress Administration produced murals promoting the New Deal. The government recruited Hollywood and New York ad agencies to promote the war effort and to convince Americans their activities at home had a direct impact on the fighting in Europe and the Pacific.

In more recent times, the government has used propaganda to promote White House initiatives. In the 1980s, the Reagan administration distributed editorials about Central America and the Small Business Administration that the Government Accountability Office called "covert propaganda." George H.W. Bush liked using prepackaged, ready-to-air news reports to tell the world how great he was, and under Clinton, that propaganda technique was used by the Department of Agriculture, the Census Bureau, and the EPA. The HHS used phony video reports to push Clinton's Medicare reform proposals. Clinton used taxpayer money to distribute self-serving videos to stations around the country. George W. Bush loved the fake news reports, and many smaller local stations aired his antidrug "reports" like they were regular staff-produced journalism and not propaganda to promote Bush's agenda.

Obama, of course, took it to a whole new level, misusing billions of taxpayer dollars for his own public relations and propaganda. Yes, billions! Presidents and Congress are masters at using "other people's money"—your money—to support their own political agendas. It's absolutely Mob-like. In a 2009 conference call, Obama's staff encouraged artists, writers, and filmmakers to support Obama initiatives on healthcare, education, and the environment, suggesting that producing propaganda would help ensure their access to lucrative National Endowment for the Arts funding. Within three days, dozens of arts groups had signed a press release endorsing Obama's healthcare plan.

It goes on and on. Obama used administrators of the Department of Education to promote his Direct Loan student financial aid program. The Justice Department had a staff troll who scurried around the internet, anonymously posting comments and shaping public opinion. White House staffers sent emails to various government agencies promoting healthcare reform, leading many career civil servants to believe they were getting direct orders from the president to support the president's agenda—or else. HHS used taxpayer money to hire Andy Griffith to promote Medicare and Obamacare on television.

It's All against the Law

None of this is legal. According to the House Oversight Committee, the Constitution prohibits it, and so does the United States Code. Laws prohibiting propaganda activities are also written into various appropriations bills. The GAO specifically prohibits public relations activities that involve "self-aggrandizement" or "puffery" or anything "designed to aid a political party or candidate."

Politicians have been concerned about propaganda for more than a hundred years. Many don't want agencies using sales pitches to extol their performance or to increase demand for government services. In 1913, they passed a law banning the use of appropriated funds "for the compensation of any publicity experts." For the last seventy years, most annual funding bills block government agencies from spending money "for publicity or propaganda."

None of these measures have worked. The law doesn't define "publicity" or "propaganda," for instance, and many agencies get around them by calling their public relations staffers by another name—public affairs specialists, communications specialists, or community affairs experts, for instance. And then there's the problem of identifying propaganda. When an agency disseminates a half-truth, it's not lying in the strictest sense. It's just trying to deceive the public.

The laws about propaganda are never enforced anyway. At least against the politicians and their government-employed henchmen. They are only enforced against you and me. The House Oversight Committee might issue a report revealing how underhanded Obama was, but no one gets fined or goes to jail or loses their funding. The GAO sometimes investigates, but only when a congressional committee asks them to, and even then, there are rarely any repercussions. The DOJ has never prosecuted anyone for violating these laws, and as a result, everyone ignores them.

That's why we have situations like we had in 2015, when the EPA proposed expanding the Clean Water Act. The proposed new rules would have a big impact on dairy farmers, home builders, timber companies, and many other industries. Thirty states expressed their concern about the new rules.

But rather than sit down with opponents to negotiate changes, the EPA instead partnered with a bunch of environmental groups and used a social media program to stuff the public record with comments supporting the stricter rules. They did this right out in the open, promoting their campaign on their websites and blogs and soliciting help from groups and prominent individuals. When the campaign was over, EPA administrator Gina McCarthy said the overpowering support for the new rules was evidence that the measure was widely supported. The GAO investigated, but there were no fines, and no one got fired.

Tax Dollars for Propaganda

Lax enforcement also explains the explosion we've seen in tax dollars going to propaganda. According to an R Street policy study from 2016, the federal government spent nearly a billion dollars on advertising and public relations contracts with the private sector in 2015 alone. Over a five-year period, it spent nearly $4 billion. When Obamacare became a reality for millions of Americans in 2013, Obama spent $700 million in taxpayer money to tell us how great his program would be. Again, your tax dollars became Obama's personal piggy bank, used to deceive you. Do you think Obama read Machiavelli's *The Prince*?

None of this includes the billions spent on salaries for federal employees hired to promote government programs and initiatives. For example, when Obama took office, he immediately created the White House Office of Digital Communications and hired a fourteen-person staff. This outfit made Wilson's Office of Public Information look like an elementary school social studies project. The WHODC turbocharged the Obamacare campaign, spinning out posts, videos, editorials, letters, and web pages promoting healthcare reform. They commandeered White House and federal Twitter feeds, making emotional appeals to voters to support the law. Alarmed opponents of Obamacare wanted to see the onslaught stopped, but, alas, federal laws prohibiting propaganda say nothing about the internet. Those laws were written a century before the internet and haven't been amended.

Donald Trump, who is no stranger to self-promotion and had a Twitter account with eighty-eight million followers before Twitter banned him from the platform, got into the propaganda act in 2020 when he proposed spending $300 million in taxpayer money on an ad campaign to cheer up an American public beaten down by the coronavirus pandemic.

The media blitz was planned by HHS spokesman Michael Caputo, a Trump loyalist, who planned to air them before the

2020 election. Dennis Quaid and CeCe Winans agreed to appear in the ads. But the ad blitz was canceled after it was revealed that Caputo had offered early vaccinations to Santa Claus performers—as well as to their elves and stage wives—who agreed to promote the vaccinations. You read that correctly. The Trump administration bribed Mrs. Claus and all those cute elves. Come on, Donald…not Santa Claus!

"There's a better label for this type of ad campaign, one that aims to stir positive emotions in contravention of the facts," Hamilton and American Enterprise scholar Kevin Kosar wrote in *Politico*. "It's called propaganda, and it's a form of communication that many Americans have trouble recognizing."

The Importance of Reliable Information

We all benefit when our government communicates with us, alerting us to when our property tax bill is due or where we can get a flu shot. We need clear, useful information about what tax forms to use or how to sign up for Medicare when we turn sixty-five. We need government websites that allow us to register our cars or apply for a backyard burning permit. Our massive government is in a position to collect enormous databases of information that help us live our lives better. We can find out what kind of skills are in high demand and how to acquire the skills to qualify for those jobs. We can check unemployment rates to find out where the jobs are and the average wage they pay. We can use Commerce Department trade statistics to make business decisions.

But we all lose when the government uses tax dollars to deceive us or convince us to support one policy over another. When the government uses half-truths or outright lies to persuade us, we lose faith in *everything* the government tells us.

COVID propaganda is the most recent example. In March 2020, Fauci told *60 Minutes* that masks were unnecessary. A few months later, he changed his tune and advocated cloth masks, claiming that he was worried that recommending N95 mask–wearing would create a mask shortage among healthcare workers, who needed the masks more. But Fauci also privately downplayed mask use. This suggests he only advocated cloth masks as a way to divert attention from surgical or N95 masks and provide a sense of hope for Americans.

Fauci's mixed messages only added to the public's confusion and generated a backlash. The end result was that some believed in masks and others felt they were an unnecessary government manipulation.

The irony about propaganda is that it is often used to reassure us. But its very use is what makes us so uneasy about our government and elected leaders.

Propaganda, like insider trading and crony capitalism, is one of those issues that's difficult for us to detect. So when we go to the Labor Department website and learn that a higher minimum wage is good for the economy and won't destroy jobs, we believe it. Until we go to the Congressional Budget Office and find out that raising the minimum wage will, in fact, eliminate a lot of jobs.

We don't know who to believe.

The sheer volume of information coming out of our sprawling government is simply staggering. The federal government manages twenty-four thousand websites. The billions the government spends each year on advertising and public relations contracts doesn't take into account the billions more we spend publishing reports and government journals. The $117 million Government Publishing Office has more than a million publications in its catalog. In 2002, the State Department had 6 people working in its public information office. By 2016, it had about 150. A report from 2012 described the department's public information operation as "a global media empire reaching a larger direct audience than the paid circulation of the ten largest newspapers in the US."

No one is arguing here against a politician's efforts to promote his or her own agenda. That's to be expected and encouraged. We have to know someone's aims before we can decide whether to vote for them.

But once they're in office, once they have the job, their duty changes. They must go from persuading people to helping people by providing clean, unvarnished information. When they pollute that information with advocacy, they lose credibility, and their constituents lose trust. That erodes the underpinnings of democracy.

What We Can Do

We don't hear much about propaganda in the media, but I think it is as pernicious as any of the Machiavellian behaviors I've already described in this book. I don't advocate stemming the flow of information coming from our government, but I am in favor of putting in safeguards to make it safer from deceit and disinformation. Some other ideas:

- We need to modernize our laws to acknowledge the internet as the primary medium for government propaganda.
- We need to put some teeth into those same laws. Agencies who abuse those laws should have to repay the money, and staffers who are responsible should face disciplinary action.
- We need to enforce our federal ethics policy. That policy is very clear: "Public service is a public trust. Each employee

has a responsibility to the United States Government and its citizens to place loyalty to the Constitution, laws and ethical principles above private gain." We need to hold our civilian workforce in the federal government to that policy so no one can question the impartiality or objectivity of those administering programs.

- We need a watchdog agency with some clout. Some government officials who acknowledge the prevalence of propaganda do little to stop the practice. In fact, they employ it themselves. For instance, the staff report issued from the House Oversight and Political Reform Committee in 2010 was crafted by Republicans and mostly attacked Democrats. Are we supposed to believe that Republicans aren't pulling the same tricks? If we want the GAO or some other agency to crack the whip, we need to enable them and give them the ammunition they need.

The rest, I'm afraid, is up to us. We must demand better.

Chapter 7

Corruption in Our Hometowns

"Democracy is not the law of the majority but the protection of the minority."

—ALBERT CAMUS

GRAFT, EXTORTION, AND PALM-GREASING IN WASHINGton, DC, get the national headlines, but the local news around the country is often rich in stories of deception and double-dealing that take place in plain sight on the steps of city hall and state capitals.

In a study at Harvard's Edmond J. Safra Center for Ethics, researchers found that more than twenty thousand public officials and private citizens were convicted of crimes related to government corruption between 1994 and 2014. The "overwhelming majority" of these crimes occurred at the state and local level. We're talking about state representatives, city council members, and the aldermen who run the small towns and county governments. That same study found that corruption is "very common" or "extremely common" in almost half the states in the US.

Keep in mind these numbers just reflect the people who got caught and convicted. The actual number of people engaging in backroom deals, payoffs, and other forms of malfeasance is much higher. To get a conviction for corruption anywhere, you need to have a strong-willed district attorney who has the time, money, and manpower to succeed, and there are only so many of those around. The result is what Sicilian movie director Frank Capra called "a political mafia."

"When you get to political machines that can control a state, then you're really into organized crime—almost," Capra said. "You're fighting a political mafia."

The Harvard study measured corruption by surveying news reporters, who sit through meetings, read information packets, and follow politicians' voting records and campaign spending. That study found that illegal corruption (more on the difference between legal and illegal corruption in a bit) is "moderately common" or "very common" in both the executive and legislative branches in a significant number of states, including California, Florida, Illinois, New Jersey, and Texas, Idaho, North and South Dakota, and the majority of the New England states—Massachusetts, Maine, New Hampshire, and Vermont—are perceived to be the least corrupt states.

The amount of corruption in any state is also related to heavy campaign spending. That makes sense. If you have to spend $170 million to become governor, you need to raise a lot of money and make a lot of promises.

Corruption is a way of life in many statehouses. Take Illinois, for example. Four of Illinois' last seven governors have gone to prison. The most notorious of this bunch was Rod Blagojevich, who was sentenced to fourteen years in prison for attempting to sell an appointment to Barack Obama's vacant seat in the US Senate and seventeen other counts of corruption.

Blagojevich, the state's fortieth governor, was really just following an Illinois tradition. His predecessor, George Ryan, also went to prison, as did Dan Walker, the thirty-sixth governor, and Otto Kerner, the thirty-third governor. One Illinois politician, a $30,000-a-year Secretary of State named Paul Powell, stuffed $800,00 in cash from bribes and payoffs into shoeboxes. A former Illinois state treasurer went to jail for defrauding banks out of several million dollars, and a former state auditor—the state's financial watchdog—paid a stiff fine for dodging questions about his campaign spending.

Now, I'm not passing judgment on the guilt or innocence of these people. Honest people can be brought up on some serious-sounding changes by their political rivals. That happens all the time. And the justice system itself can be corrupt. But as voters and taxpayers and citizens of this country, we are constantly being pulled in one direction or the other, and the result is we stop trusting anyone.

Illinois is home to Chicago, which also has a rich tradition of fraud and racketeering. Chicago was home to Al Capone and scores of other Mob figures, and the local politicians seem to have learned a lot from organized crime. In the 1990s, for instance, the FBI's Operation Silver Shovel uncovered labor union corruption, drug trafficking, and other organized crime activities that sent eighteen public officials to jail, including six aldermen. In the 1980s, the FBI and IRS combined forces to root out corruption in Chicago's Cook County court system. Ninety-two people were convicted, including fifteen judges, after a three-year undercover operation. According to the Illinois Policy Institute, federal prosecutors in the judicial district covering Chicago and northern Illinois have obtained 1,731 convictions since 1976.

Despite its rich heritage of corruption, Illinois really can't compete with Kentucky when it comes to malfeasance. In 2014, two academic studies attempted to determine which states were the most corrupt. One study analyzed criminal convictions while another surveyed longtime statehouse reporters for the news media. Both studies reached the same conclusion: Kentucky politicians are as crooked as they come.

In Kentucky, politicians give their friends $50,000-a-year jobs that they don't have to show up for. We did this all the time in the Mob; we held union "no show" jobs that we could hand out to our friends and relatives so they could get paid for a job they never worked. Kentucky has taken this practice to the next level. They illegally award state contracts to their political supporters. State officials routinely take kickbacks in exchange for funneling state contracts to outside firms. In the 1990s, fifteen state legislators, including the Speaker of the House, went to prison for taking bribes to support horse-racing legislation in the state. What stood out about that scandal was how inexpensive it was to buy Kentucky's politicians. One state senator sold her vote for $2,000, and others sold out for $3,000. Men and women, Democrat and Republican. Money talks, I guess, even a small amount of it. I wish the politicians I bribed had come this cheap.

In places like Kentucky and Illinois, racketeering is simply a political way of life. It's shot through every level of government, from the legislative branch to the judicial and executive. Everyone does it because they assume everyone else is also doing it. Some local politicians learn the tricks of the trade in their statehouses early in their careers and then carry their knowledge and practices to Congress.

Let's use Dan Rostenkowski as an example of this. Rostenkowski was born and raised in Chicago's political world. His dad was a longstanding alderman in a largely Polish Chicago district, and he grew up listening to precinct captains bellow late into the night during party meetings in the living room. Rostenkowski was elected to the state legislature when he was twenty-four. After being elected to Congress several years later, he became adept at funneling federal funds back home, and over his long career, he rose to become one of the most powerful Democrats in Congress.

In 1994, Rostenkowski got tangled in a corruption investigation headed by future US Attorney Eric Holder. Rostenkowski was accused of hiring "ghost" employees—people paid for jobs they never did (again, Mob-like)—using congressional funds to buy gifts for political supporters, tampering with Grand Jury witnesses, and using federal funds to pay for his personal car. In 1996, he went to prison for fifteen months.

But what Rostenkowski did was fairly commonplace in Congress, and many fellow politicians had to admit it. "He took the hit for the whole House for practices that were there since time immemorial," said Congressman Bill Frenzel of Minnesota in Richard Cohen's 2000 book *The Pursuit of Power and the End of the Old Politics*. Former president Gerald Ford wrote one pardon letter after leaving office, and he wrote it for Rostenkowski.

"Danny's problem was he played precisely under the rules of the city of Chicago," Ford later said in Thomas DeFrank's 2007 book, *Write It When I'm Gone: Remarkable Off-the-Record Conversations with Gerald R. Ford*. "Now, those aren't the same rules that any other place in the country lives by, but in Chicago they were totally legal, and Danny got a screwing."

Corruption like that, practiced by Rostenkowski and untold others, is so common that researchers have started to break it into two different categories. *Legal corruption* (or institutional corruption) is when a politician accepts a contribution or political support in return for an unspoken promise to help the contributor in some way. Although the two actions are related, it's not illegal because there is no direct quid pro quo. *Illegal corruption* is when a politician gets cash or gifts in return for helping special interests. The two are almost impossible to distinguish sometimes, but they work together to undermine our trust in our government. And they say mobsters are masters of deceit? I'd say the politicians are taking the trophy these days.

Why Corruption Is Bad

By now, we should all be fed up with corruption at any level of government. Not only is it criminal and fraudulent misuse of our tax dollars and public trust, but it's also killing our economy.

Several different studies have shown that corruption decreases economic growth. It scares away investors looking for a place to expand their companies or start new ones. In Illinois, one think tank estimated the state loses about $550 million a year to corruption—which amounts to almost $10 billion from 2000 to 2017. This prevents nearly three hundred thousand Illinois residents who are actively seeking work from finding jobs, the study found.

According to the Illinois Policy Institute, states with higher levels of red tape and corruption have higher levels of residents moving elsewhere. Pay declines as fewer new businesses move in, and existing businesses avoid expansions or innovations. In Illinois, the result is a state economic growth rate that's less than half the national average.

Corruption also helps explain why Illinois has the slowest economic growth of the five most populous states in the country. When you look at all fifty states, those like Illinois with slower economic growth and lower production also have the highest levels of corruption convictions. Corruption causes governments to become more cumbersome as elected officials insert exemptions and sweetheart deals into local ordinances, and resulting complexity increases corruption even more. The result is an economy that is bound up and stagnant.

Kentucky and New Mexico—considered the fifth most corrupt state in the US—also have lackluster economic growth. Too often, local politicians simply have too much power. In some municipalities, aldermen and commissioners can micromanage things like zoning variances and building permits. This gives the pols uncounted opportunities to put the squeeze on businesses and entrepreneurs.

This kind of behavior is a cornerstone of the Mafia's extortion operation. As recently as 2021, the feds in New York prosecuted the leadership of the Colombo crime family for extorting money from a Queens labor union. My old family was accused of shaking down the union for more than twenty years, assuming control of key contracting and union businesses, with a lucrative side scam in fake construction safety certificates, marijuana trafficking, and loan-sharking.

For the Mob, this kind of activity is illegal. Not so for the politicians.

Unbelievably, in many jurisdictions, lawmakers are also property tax appeals attorneys. This is straight out of the Mafia how-to guide. The tax assessor raises the tax assessment on an office building in the city, and the property owner then has to hire the lawmaker's tax firm to get the bill reduced. When you run the city and oversee its operations and employees, it's not particularly difficult to get a tax assessment lowered. In places like Illinois, the aldermen who do property tax appeals also work hand-in-glove with the corrupt tax assessor. Some city leaders earn millions of dollars for their firms through this rigged system.

Corruption is typically worse in states that have cumbersome and highly restrictive governments. When a developer or a business owner is hobbled by red tape, sometimes the cheapest and most effective option is for them to bribe officials for regulatory favors, permits, subsidies, or government contracts. We did this in New York all the time. That's why former Kentucky state representative Keith Hall was convicted of bribing a mine inspector to overlook violations at a coal mine Hall owned. It's why federal corruption convictions are 8 percent more common in Illinois than in any other state.

Why Should We Care about Corruption?

Although economists have shown that corruption hurts economic growth, most Americans believe bribery, fraud, embezzlement, and extortion in our government is insignificant. In other countries, dictators steal millions while their subjects die from hunger. In our country, politicians pad their bank accounts and help out their friends and business partners. By comparison, it doesn't seem so bad, right?

Wrong.

While the corruption in local government might seem minor in comparison to oligarchies and third-world dictatorships, even small-scale corrupt practices can have a tremendous impact on a community. Citizens lose faith in their elected officials and distrust their government. Citizens wonder if they are expected to donate to campaigns or provide special favors for the administrator reviewing their permit application. Should they offer bribes? Will they get caught and go to jail if they do? Will their business lose to competitors who know how to play the game of graft? If you asked these entrepreneurs and business owners, they'd tell you that they'd rather pay higher taxes than be forced to participate in a dishonest and unpredictable system.

Michael W. Hail, an associate professor of government at Morehead State University, said average citizens in many parts of the country have come to expect unethical behavior from their elected officials and government employees. They think it's the norm. But it's not, Hail says. It's a rigged system that's against the law, and people must be aware of that.

Corruption and Term Limits

The longer a politician serves in office, the more their influence grows and the more exposure they have to special interests. They also face more elections and need more campaign money. This might explain why voters across the country have repeatedly favored term limits. It might also explain why politicians keep fighting term limits.

Take Arkansas, for instance. Voters there love term limits. In 1992, they passed a term limits referendum with about 70 percent of the vote. Twelve years later, when the politicians tried to double those terms, the people rejected the move with about 70 percent of the vote again.

ZSo the politicians devised something called the Arkansas Ethics Transparency and Financial Reform Amendment. It was a twenty-two-page constitutional amendment, and hidden in it was a repeal of the state's term limits and a pay raise for lawmakers. Since the 2014 bill's title was misleading—who's not in favor of ethics transparency?—the measure slipped past voters and passed with 52 percent of the vote.

Since then, seven Arkansas state legislators responsible for the amendment have been convicted of bribery or fraud, including the mastermind of the amendment, a senator named John

Woods. Woods was sentenced to nearly twenty years in prison for organizing and leading a bribery scheme in which state funds were directed to nonprofits in exchange for kickbacks.

Not all politicians opposed to term limits are criminals, of course. But many politicians who promise to voluntarily limit their terms, even when the law doesn't require it, often renege on their promise. Sen. Susan Collins of Maine promised in 1996 to serve only two terms. She's on her fifth. Markwayne Mullin of Oklahoma promised to limit his service, but broke that promise when the time came, declaring that "God told me to break my term limits pledge." Yeah, right. This is hypocrisy. It's also Machiavellian. "A prince never lacks legitimate reasons to break his promise," Machiavelli wrote. "The promise given was a necessity of the past; the word broken is a necessity of the present." It's commonplace for politicians to break their promises when it comes to term limits. Arizona State Representative Diego Rodriguez pledged to support term limits in Congress but voted against them on the House floor.

Family Matters

One reason politicians like to stay in office is that it gives them more opportunities to misuse campaign contributions.

Duncan Hunter of California is a good example. Hunter used campaign funds to finance his luxury lifestyle and to pay for five extramarital affairs. He took vacations to Italy and flew his family's pet rabbit across the country in first class. Yes, you read that correctly. His "pet rabbit" flew first class on taxpayers' dimes. When was the last time many of you flew first class? Hunter, a Republican from California, entered Congress in 2013, just four years after his father left Congress following a twenty-eight-year career. Hunter might still be in office, but his wife pleaded guilty to corruption, and Hunter eventually pleaded guilty to misusing campaign funds. He was packing his bags to go to jail when Trump pardoned him in January 2020.

Maxine Waters, a thirty-year veteran of Congress, has been accused of using her office to enrich her family through sophisticated kickback schemes. Her daughter, for instance, runs an outfit that does mailings for Waters. The *Los Angeles Times* reported that Waters' relatives pocketed more than a million dollars over the course of eight years from businesses and political campaigns that were in some way connected to Waters. In 2010, Waters was charged with violating House ethics rules after it was reported that she had used her connections to insure a $12 million federal bailout of OneUnited Bank, which had contributed heavily to her campaign and in which her husband owned stock. The ethics charges were dropped two years later, although Waters' chief of staff, who is also her grandson, was given a letter of reprimand. Meanwhile, thanks to the bailout of OneUnited, Waters' husband was able to protect the hundreds of thousands he had invested in the bank.

When we talk about politicians who use their influence to help their relatives, we can't overlook Joe Biden. When Biden was vice president, his son Hunter somehow got a lucrative position with Burisma Holdings, owned by a Ukrainian oligarch. Hunter was pulling down up to $50,000 a month on this deal. At the same time, his dad was supposed to be fighting corruption in Ukraine. Even Hunter's partner, the stepson of John Kerry, was opposed to Hunter's position with Burisma because of the damage the arrangement would do to their reputations.

Of course, nothing happened to Hunter or to Joe Biden. The mainstream media buried this story during Biden's campaign, and he went on to win the presidency. Hunter, meanwhile, wrote books, sold artwork for millions, and continued his dirty dealings with China.

But no one looked after their family as well as Harry Reid, the longtime Democratic senator from Nevada. Somebody should write a book on this guy. Reid served five terms in the Senate, and year after year, he made the conservative public-integrity nonprofit Judicial Watch's Most Corrupt Politician list.

In 2012, Reid was involved in an influence-peddling scandal involving a Chinese "green energy" firm represented by Reid's son's law firm. The next year, Reid took money from the convicted Nevada developer Harvey Whittemore, who also hired four of Reid's sons. That same year, Reid sponsored nearly $50 million in earmarks that benefited clients of another one of his sons. Reid was pretty close to being exposed before he suddenly announced his retirement from the Senate. But before he left, he managed to expedite a $115 million foreign investor visa deal for another son's casino client. According to the Judicial Watch, Reid got the Department of Homeland Security to override agency procedures to rush through hundreds of visa applications from foreign nationals who helped fund a Las Vegas hotel and casino that hired Rory Reid to provide legal representation.

Reid, a former boxer, learned the ropes while serving in local office. Before running for the Senate, he was the city attorney in Henderson, Nevada, an assemblyman for the state, and then lieutenant governor. Later, he served on the state Gaming Control Board, which was established to keep Nevada's gambling industry on the up and up and free of Mob influences.

Ironically, before Reid made a fortune for his family in the US Senate, he made a name for himself *fighting* corruption. In the late 1970s, when entertainment manager and businessman Jack Gordon offered Reid a $12,000 bribe to get approval for some new casino games, Reid alerted the FBI. The FBI taped the bribery attempt, and when they stepped in to arrest Gordon, Reid jumped Gordon and started choking him. "You son of a bitch," Reid shouted angrily, "you tried to bribe me!"

The incident became a significant entry in Reid's career timeline, but to me, it's just another laughable example of Machiavelli's influence. Machiavelli advised princes to carefully craft a public image that would hide their true nature. "Everyone sees what you appear to be," he wrote in *The Prince*, "(but) few experience what you really are." The Jack Gordon bribery story suggests Reid was a righteous, crusading public servant, too pure to be corrupted by money. But the reality was something altogether different.

Chapter 8

Growth and Breakdowns

"The most terrifying words in the English language are: I'm from the government, and I'm here to help."

—RONALD REAGAN

THOMAS JEFFERSON ONCE SAID, "MY READING OF HISTORY convinces me that most bad government results from too much government."

Jefferson wasn't alone in thinking this. Our founding fathers were very clear on how they felt about big government: they hated it. They had just won a bloody and hard-fought victory over an oppressive government. In framing our constitution, they were determined to create a blueprint for a smaller, less intrusive government that would serve the people's needs while exerting as little control over their lives as possible. It would be a government run by the people for the people—and *not* for the benefit of elected officials.

But in recent years, the United States government has experienced unprecedented growth. Economist and financial analyst Gary Shilling calculated that 53 percent of Americans are now dependent on the government for "major parts of their income." That's 161 million people.

"If these goodies were taken away, these people would be very unhappy," Shilling told C-SPAN.

These recipients include teachers, soldiers, bureaucrats, and other government employees; welfare and social security recipients; Medicare recipients; college students living off student loans; government pensioners; public housing beneficiaries; and people who work for government contractors. That number also includes the recipients' dependents. Shilling also counted all the attorneys, accountants, and professionals who make a living helping citizens deal with federal agencies, like the IRS. Shilling estimated that if the government expansion continues at its current pace, soon an astounding 67 percent of Americans could be dependent on the government for their livelihood. The government will have direct control over the lives of more than two-thirds of the nation.

Is this what Jefferson had in mind when he worried about "too much" government? I think it's exactly what he had in mind.

And make no mistake: control is what corruption is all about. It's what the Mafia is all about. We wanted leverage on everybody, and in our heyday, we had it. We controlled the unions. We controlled major categories of commerce, manufacturing, entertainment, and transportation. We controlled elections, and we controlled large blocs of the voting public.

The True Size of Government

When we talk about the size of government, it's easy to get lost in the different ways it's measured.

If you're just talking about the number of federal employees, you're not getting the full picture. That number has been capped by federal law at 2 million since the 1950s, and it rarely fluctuates far from that. So even though government spending is skyrocketing and the federal deficit is astronomical—something we'll talk about in the next chapter—that money isn't going to hire full-time permanent federal workers.

Instead, it's going toward hiring workers through contracts and grants, and those numbers are obscene. In 2020, we had 2.2 million federal employees, 1.4 million military personnel, and over half a million postal workers. But we also had 5 million federal contract workers. On top of that, we had 1.8 million people hired through grants, one of the highest numbers in recent history. The only time it was higher was in 2010, after the government pumped billions into the economy to respond to the Great Recession.

When you hear pundits talk about the "blended" federal workforce, this is what they are talking about—soldiers, bureaucrats, letter carriers, contract workers, and people hired through grants. Contract workers include clerical, food-service, and maintenance staff hired through outsourcing, and federal grant workers come from law enforcement, universities, research labs, and a whole host of nonprofits and small businesses.

And that's just the federal workforce. When you add in state and local government workers, there are about 25 million people on the government payroll. That's 15 percent of the entire workforce.

When Barack Obama entered office at the height of the recession, the blended federal workforce stood at 10 million civil servants. The number grew to 11.3 million, but Obama got the number down to 9 million before leaving office.

Donald Trump came in promising to drain the swamp, but it didn't turn out that way. Although he left political and Cabinet posts vacant, he added more than 2 million jobs to the blended federal workforce, even while grousing about "duplication and redundancy everywhere" and "billions and billions" of wasted tax dollars.

"You know we have so many people in government, even me, I look at some of the jobs and it's people over people over people," he said after being in office for a month. "There are hundreds and hundreds of jobs that are totally unnecessary jobs."

To his credit, Trump's staff developed dozens of reorganization plans, but Congress wouldn't listen because Trump's plan called for cutting jobs and "reskilling" workers. I'm not sure why, but the Democrats wanted nothing to do with that. Maybe they didn't want to lose the support of the unions; I don't know. Read the rest of this chapter, and tell me what *you* think.

Enter the Unions

You can't talk about a growing government without talking about public employee unions. These unions have played a major role in the growth of government.

When I was in the Mob, we controlled most of the private-sector unions. We borrowed money from their pension funds, and we used our influence over them as leverage to get what we wanted. If you were a developer in New York, you had to deal with unions, which meant you had to deal with us. If you needed to keep the unions out of your project to turn a profit, you had to kick back some of those savings to us in return for keeping picketers off your construction site.

Today, those private-sector unions for carpenters, mechanics, electricians, bricklayers, truck drivers, and other blue-collar jobs are a shadow of what they once were. In 1955, for instance, organized labor represented a third of all blue-collar workers who didn't work on farms. Today, only one in ten workers are represented by unions.

Public-sector unions are a different story altogether. Back in the thirties and forties, most economists, labor leaders, and politicians—including pro-union Democrats like Franklin Roosevelt—opposed unions for public-sector employees. If these police, firefighters, and trash collectors had unions, they argued, they could cripple the government until the government met their demands. This was "unthinkable and intolerable," Roosevelt said.

Here's how one New York Supreme Court judge explained the problem of public-sector unions:

> To tolerate or recognize any combination of civil service employees of the government as a labor organization or union is not only incompatible with the spirit of democracy, but inconsistent with every principle upon which our government is founded.

> Nothing is more dangerous to public welfare than to admit that hired servants of the State can dictate to the government the hours, the wages, and conditions under which they will carry on essential services vital to the welfare, safety, and security of the citizen. To admit as true that government employees have power to halt or check the functions of government unless their demands are satisfied is to transfer to them all legislative, executive, and judicial power. Nothing would be more ridiculous.

Well, guess what! As ridiculous as it is, that's exactly what happened. And we can thank the Democrats for it.

The Democrat-Union Alliance

Throughout the 1950s and 1960s, Democrats joined the private-sector unions to defeat Republican efforts to weaken collective bargaining. Before long, union workers became the foot soldiers in the Democrats' election campaigns. Unions raised money for Democratic candidates and walked the neighborhoods to support Democratic initiatives. In return, Democrats made sure the unions got what they wanted.

As private-sector unions began to fade, the Democrats set their sights on a powerful new partner: public-sector unions. In 1958, New York City was the first to give city employees collective bargaining rights, and in 1962, President John Kennedy did the same for federal workers. Public-sector unions soon spread like wildfire across the land. In 1967, nearly four hundred thousand local-government employees became unionized in New York state alone. By 2009, public-sector teachers, librarians, trash collectors, policemen, firefighters, and other government workers outnumbered private-sector union members.

Today, the 1.5 million members of the American Federation of Teachers is bigger than the largest private-sector union (United Food and Commercial Workers). Still, the AFT is less than half the size of the largest labor union in the United States—the 3.2-million-member National Education Association.

The growth of public-sector unions has given government workers incredible clout. They stuff Democrats' campaigns with contributions, which essentially allows them to pick who their future bosses will be. Not only can they handpick the person who will sit opposite them at the bargaining table, but they can sit down at the table with an already sizable number of bargaining chips thanks to the campaign favors their candidates owe them.

But the unions don't stop there. They can demand incredible pension benefits, higher wages, lenient working conditions, and a protected workforce. That's why thousands of police officers in states like New York and Massachusetts earn more than their governors do, and why, according to the *New York Times*, unionized government workers earn fourteen dollars more per hour than their private-sector counterparts. That's why the city of Buffalo had the same size workforce in 2006 as it did in 1950, even though it's population was half the size.

Union Demands Expand Government

Public-sector union demands often lead to higher taxes and more government spending. As political scientist Daniel DiSalvo pointed out in the magazine *National Affairs* in 2010, these unions also work to expand government.

For example, the correctional officers' union in California used its considerable clout to convince the state to build more prisons. Between 1980 and 2000, the number of California prisons increased from twelve to thirty-four, which of course increased the demand for prison guards and solidified the union's power in the state.

The correctional officers' union also pushed for tougher sentencing that caused prison populations to skyrocket, thus requiring even more guards. You've got to give these guys some credit for how they feathered their nest. By 2020, the average union member prison guard made nearly $80,000 a year and well over $100,000 with overtime. That's twice the national average. It's a lousy job—I got to know a lot of prison guards over the years I was behind bars, and I would never want to be one—but they can retire at fifty with a pension equal to 90 percent of their salary. Lousy job, but it has a sweet payback; you get to pressure lawmakers to pass laws to pay you more and allow you to hire more people on the taxpayers' dimes.

Other people's money. What's more, what impact are these laws having on our minority populations, who have a disproportionate number being sent to prison? Democrats are the biggest hypocrites. From one side of their mouths, they preach equal opportunity; from the other, they back tough-on-crime laws that send even more minorities to prison.

Public-sector unions might ultimately topple our government with pension plans like that. The sweet deal prison guards get in California is common for public-sector union workers across the country. As a result, dozens of states are facing huge pension payouts that they don't have the money to cover. The unfunded pension and healthcare costs for retiring public-sector employees across the country exceeds $1 trillion. In California alone, it exceeds $90 billion.

What does all this mean? Well, it means you and I are going to have to pay more in taxes and get fewer government services. As DiSalvo pointed out, most states' pension commitments are constitutionally guaranteed, and "there is no easy way out of this financial sinkhole."

"If the government must spend more on pensions, it cannot spend more on schools, roads, and relief for the poor—in other words, the basic functions people expect their governments to perform," DiSalvo said.

Modeled on the Mob

Unions are a good example of how our government has become a Mafia Democracy. Just like the Mob, elected officials saw that cozying up to unions could help them gain leverage and push their agenda for expanding government. It worked! The problem is that they also brought our states closer to insolvency and reduced the quality of the government service we get.

The stereotype for a government worker is that he is lazy, unskilled, unmotivated, and indifferent to the needs of the taxpayer. Is that true? I can't say, but people who study this stuff believe it is—and they blame the unions. In private industry, workers are eager to get you to fill out a survey and tell them how well they served you. When's the last time a government worker asked you to do that?

Other studies have shown that government workers do not enjoy their work as much as people in private enterprise. According to one study by the Brookings Institute, "federal employees trail private-sector employees on almost every measure of their work." They don't have as many resources to get their jobs done. They don't feel their talents are valued. They have lower job satisfaction. They don't trust their supervisors as much. Morale is low.

Although lower-end union workers might earn more than their contemporaries in private industry, most talented and ambitious workers wouldn't dream of working in a bloated bureaucracy, where the work is rote and advancement occurs at a glacial pace. That means the government appeals more to what New York University professor Paul Light calls "the security-craver" and not the risk-takers who excel in today's business world. The result is a government workforce that is unimaginative and plodding, and a public that has little confidence in them to do a good job.

Breakdowns Increasing

Confidence in our government rises and falls with the economy, but it's also heavily influenced by what political scientists call "government breakdowns." Breakdowns are basically when the government tries to tackle a big problem and falls on its face, such as when Obama tried to launch a website for Obamacare and it didn't work, or when George W. Bush left thousands stranded in New Orleans after Hurricane Katrina. The Great Recession, prompted by the government's weak oversight of the shady dealings of banks and mortgage companies, was another major breakdown. Can you blame inflexible and indifferent government workers for these breakdowns? Probably not. But they certainly contributed.

Unfortunately, there have been a lot of government breakdowns, and they are increasing. Before 9/11, presidential administrations averaged 1.4 breakdowns per year. Reagan had four breakdowns in his two terms, and George H.W. Bush had five in his only term. Clinton had fourteen in two terms, and George W. had twenty-five, such as when Homeland Security manipulated the US terrorism warning system for political reasons and failed to stop abuses at Walter Reed Army Medical Center. Obama had twenty-eight breakdowns, including the massive Gulf of Mexico oil spill, the Edward Snowden NSA security leak, the Flint, Michigan drinking-water crisis, and the time the Centers for Disease Control mishandled anthrax and avian flu samples. The Trump administration had the Postal Service crash, the family-separation border policy failures, and Russian interference in the elections.

This isn't me just picking events and calling them breakdowns. There are people, such as the late Paul Volcker, the former chairman of the Federal Reserve Board, and scholar Paul Light, who measure this kind of stuff. Volcker worked for Carter, Reagan, and Obama and led two National Commissions on the Public Service. He was a great and widely respected man who could work with both conservatives and progressives, and he had a keen interest in making government work better. He wanted to rebuild trust, attract better workers to federal service, and help presidential appointees work better with career civil servants. He wanted to attract the cream of the crop. He wanted to restore our confidence in our government by getting the best people to deliver public policies for the nation.

"What we need is attention—much more attention—to the 'nuts and bolts' of management within the government," Volcker said in 2015, four years before he died at the age of ninety-two. "Without it, the fate of our great democracy is increasingly precarious."

I agree. I also agree with Volcker's colleague Light, who said a more effective government is a bipartisan issue. All the break-downs Light has been documenting over the years are costing money and lives and discouraging talented young people from working for the government. Who wants to work with a slog-ging, unproductive, suffocating behemoth when sharp, brisk operators like Amazon and Google are hiring?

"Americans trust their government less and less, yet it is obvi-ous we must rely on government to keep us safe from terrorism, to respond to natural disasters, and to monitor the safety of our food and cars," Light said after he and Volcker formed the nonprofit, nonpartisan Volcker Alliance to continue the work they started with the national commission. "It's time for all of us not just to collectively demand better performance from our federal government but also to do what's necessary to improve its management."

The Problem with a Growing Government

When I look at this problem of a huge and still-growing gov-ernment, I have to wonder how we're going to pay for all this control and dependency. By raising taxes on "millionaires and billionaires" the way every liberal politician in the country advocates? Look at Alexandria Ocasio-Cortez's stunt at the Met Gala in New York City in 2021 wearing a dress emblazoned with "Tax the Rich" on it. Brave move? Not really. It was more hypocritical than anything. Here is our very own Democratic socialist accepting a $35,000 ticket to an event overflowing with hideously rich elites. Is *that* how you tax the rich? Not exactly.

Although spending cuts would help quell the growth of government, neither Congress nor the White House has the backbone to inflict that kind of pain on the 99 percent of citizens across America. Pulling back entitlements and services for people is death at the voting booths for elected officials.

Instead, our elected leaders need to identify all duplication and overlap in our massive bureaucracy and reduce it. We have to stop passing major legislation and issuing executive orders without any plan for implementing it. We need to streamline. Should our frontline healthcare workers have to wade through eighteen layers of the Department of Health and Human Services to get personal protection equipment from the Strategic National Stockpile? Should small businesses be forced to pick their way through sixteen layers of the Treasury Department to get Paycheck Protection support? When your loved one is in a skilled nursing facility, should you be forced to navigate the nineteen layers of bureaucracy that separate the Department of Health and Human Services and the division of nursing homes at the Centers for Medicare and Medicaid Services?

Government bloat starts at the top. Trump did what he could to streamline, but big government has too much power and directs much of that power to sustaining its obesity. In 1981, only one cabinet secretary had a chief of staff. By 2020, fourteen of the fifteen secretaries had them. What's more, many also had a deputy chief of staff, a chief of staff to the deputy secretary, a deputy chief of staff to the deputy secretary, assistant and associate deputy secretaries, and so on and so on. I'm not making this stuff up. In the summer of 2020, there were more than a thousand deputy assistant secretaries at the executive level and 113 cabinet staffers walking around with the title of "deputy undersecretary."

This has got to stop.

When you look at the number of jobs and entitlements provided by the government, it's no surprise that the late Charles B. Shuman, former president of the Illinois Agriculture Association, once said, "The greatest threat to the future of our nation—to our freedom—is not foreign military aggression... but the growing dependence of the people on a paternalistic government."

Some people think of a paternalistic government as one that has its citizens' best interests in mind, such as when it requires that we all wear seat belts. That's a good thing.

But let's not forget that paternalism also interferes with our liberty and autonomy. When the federal government forces us to get state-sponsored health insurance, for example, we can start to feel it is controlling us and restricting our freedom. We're treated like children. I don't respond well to that, and I'm not alone.

The Mafia used paternalism too. We took control of people's lives and businesses. Sometimes we used intimidation, but just as often, we pretended to be kindhearted and helpful. Do you want protection for your bodega from street thugs? We'll protect you for a cut of your income. Do you need a quick loan? We've got you covered. This is how we wormed our way into people's lives and their livelihoods—pretending we had their best interests in mind and then manipulating them into being under our control.

Does that sound like the government to you? It does to me too.

This is the Mafia Democracy.

Chapter 9

Wasteful Spending

"As quickly as you start spending federal money in large amounts, it looks like free money."

—DWIGHT D. EISENHOWER

WHEN GEORGE W. BUSH TOOK OFFICE IN 2001, THE national debt was $5.8 trillion. It had taken the US more than two hundred years, two world wars, a depression, and a recession to fall into that gaping hole, and for many Americans, enough was enough. Regular citizens can't spend money they don't have (or don't intend to pay back), so why should the federal government?

Well, the truth was that our federal folks were just getting warmed up. During his eight years in office, Bush and Congress doubled the national debt to $11.7 trillion. Then Obama arrived for his two terms and added another $8.6 trillion to the national debt. Even Donald Trump, who only had one term in office and portrayed himself as a fiscal conservative, managed to add $6.7 trillion to the national debt.

Two months into Joe Biden's first term, on the heels of his

plan to spend nearly $2 trillion on his post-pandemic economic stimulus and another $2 trillion on infrastructure, the national debt hit an all-time record of $28 trillion and was likely to just keep getting larger. Our national debt, when measured as a percentage of the gross domestic product, is as high as it was during World War II, when people had to plant backyard "victory gardens" so they had food to eat. We are pretty much ignoring this astounding rise in debt. Just months after Biden signed the $2 trillion economic aid package, his people were back with a plan to spend $3 trillion to fight climate change and improve American manufacturing and high-technology industries.

When the Democrats are in power, they spend. When the Republicans are in power, they spend. When either party is out of power, their opponents' spending is irresponsible and will leave a disastrous debt for future generations to dig out from under.

Our Friends the Chinese

This is one area where our government *doesn't* act like the Mob. The Mob didn't borrow money. We *made* money, and then we loaned it out at impossible vigs. When people couldn't pay us back, we took over their businesses and other assets and made them our own. When you look at it this way, our government is like the schlubs we used to loanshark to. The gangsters in this scenario are the people loaning our government the money.

I'm talking now about the Chinese.

As I write this, we owe China about $1.1 trillion. The only country with a higher stake in our debt is Japan, which owns $1.2 trillion of our debt. When Trump was president and started a trade war, China's exports declined, and they were less able to buy up US Treasury bills, notes, and bonds, which is why a lot of us applauded Trump's effort to call China's bluff on trade.

So why is China, which is not exactly our ally the way Japan is, pumping so much loot into the US economy? Simple: buying Treasury notes raises the value of the dollar compared to Chinese currency, and that makes Chinese exports cheaper than American-made goods. This increases sales, increases China's income, and gives China even more cash to buy up our debt. In this sense, China has latched on to us like a monstrous leech and is sucking out our lifeblood. And politicians like Joe Biden and Barack Obama are playing right into their hands by continually increasing our national debt.

You can see how China is taking advantage of our federal government's limitless passion for borrowing and spending. China is capitalizing, just like I did when I'd loan a guy more money than he could ever pay back and then latch on to whatever business he ran and make it my own. The Mob did this *all the time*. We were experts at it. China makes us look like rank amateurs.

So what happens if China calls in its debt and starts selling its Treasury holdings? It doesn't take an economist to see that the demand for the dollar would plummet and our interest rates and prices would rise. Our economic growth would slow to a crawl. If it wanted to, China could inflict a financial crisis on us that would make The Great Recession feel like a stubbed toe.

Luckily, China doesn't want that—for now. China's economy would also suffer if our economy collapsed. But what happens if China fortifies its hold on other Asian markets and manages to increase domestic demands for its goods? What if it doesn't really need the US anymore? Well, if that happens—and don't think for a minute that China isn't already working to make that happen—then China would have tremendous leverage over us.

They could put themselves in a position to dictate terms to us that we would be too weak to refuse. This is Mob Behavior 101, people, and it's what China is doing to our country.

Don't get me wrong. I'm not saying that China is about to flip a switch and trigger an economic collapse in our country. Our economies are too interwoven. But at the same time, we need to be aware of China's existential threat to our way of life. China has become the largest economy in the world. It became the world's biggest exporter in 2009. But it still has a low standard of living, and until that changes, don't expect China to call in its vig.

Deficits Are No Big Deal, Right?

Deficit spending falls right in line with so-called modern monetary theory, which states that deficits are meaningless for countries like ours that print their own currency. This theory holds that as long as interest rates are lower than inflation rates, politicians should be free to spend away.

Really? When I hear that, I agree with guys like Thomas W. Smith, the chairman of OpenTheBooks.com, who says, "That is not a theory. It is idle wordplay, and the victim of such sophistry is the American taxpayer."

I'm not saying investing in economic recovery and infrastructure is a bad thing. Investing in better roads, bridges, dams, electrical infrastructure, and stuff like that pays returns over a long period of time. This is what we count on the government to do.

The problem I have with all this spending is that it's being done by the federal government. Their track record for spending wisely is deplorable. Lawmakers don't even know where the money goes. In 2020, the Congressional spending plan ran

5,593 pages and was sent to the Senate two hours before the vote. You'd have to be able to read forty-seven pages per minute to get through a document like that, so it's safe to assume that all those lawmakers who voted for it had no idea what was in it.

It's almost like the government is *designed* to be wasteful. The biggest spending period of the year is the last month of the fiscal year, when agencies scramble to spend their budgeted funds or risk having their budgets reduced the next year. One out of every nine dollars in federal contracts is spent in the last week of the fiscal year. In 2018, for instance, sixty-seven federal agencies spent $97 billion in the last two days of the fiscal year, buying China tableware, workout equipment, golf carts, musical instruments, and lobster tails and crab. Why doesn't Joe Biden take all *that* cash and pave roads and build electrical grids instead of running deficits? Is that so hard?

No Incentive to Cut Costs

There are fundamental reasons why our federal government wastes so much money. For starters, there is scant oversight. In any situation where there's no oversight, the original mission fades into self-aggrandizement and corruption. There is no profit motive, no incentive to cut costs, and no concern with declining productivity.

And then there are the problems with the incredible size and complexity of government. It's a sloppy, wasteful behemoth. We see signs of this all the time. In 2018, the Department of Health and Human Services made $86.5 billion in improper payments. You'd think that kind of astonishing ineptitude would have triggered some kind of overhaul or at least an investigation, right? Not so much. The next year, HHS improperly distributed $106.7 billion.

The federal government also likes to routinely send checks to dead people. In 2018, dead people received $871.9 million in Medicaid, social security, federal pension checks, and farm subsidies. The simple failure to verify deaths costs the federal government nearly $3 billion a year.

This kind of waste is not inherent. When government officials pay attention and tighten the screws, they can reduce that waste. In 2018, for example, the Education Department overpaid college students $6 billion in PELL grants. The next year, they were able to reduce that to $1.1 billion—still bad, but far better than the previous year. So, we know how to do it. We just lack the courage in Congress to make it happen.

Earmarks and Pork Barrels

When I was in the Mafia, we always took care of our neighborhoods. People knew who we were, and we wanted the people to feel safe and free to come to us if they had a problem. We kept the riffraff out, and when neighborhood people came into our clubs or restaurants, we always treated them well. We ran the numbers, and everybody—particularly the women and grandmothers—loved to play. Machiavelli preached the importance of earning the goodwill of your neighbors and followers, and we took this principle seriously. We never took advantage of the people in our neighborhoods.

Our elected leaders try to do the same thing—only they do it by doling out tax dollars to special interests back home.

Take, for instance, earmarks. Earmarks are when elected leaders siphon funds to specific projects or organizations, usually in their home districts. The process circumvents the executive branch of government, and earmarks usually only benefit what the Congressional Research Service calls "a very limited number of individuals or entities" and not the greater good. There is no objective finding of need. There's no competitive process to make sure the money goes to the most deserving project. The money is just doled out by politicians to their friends and backers.

While earmarks may benefit a larger swath of the population, pork-barrel legislation is more narrowly focused. Pork, according to the Citizens Against Government Waste, is typically requested by just one chamber of Congress. It's not competitively awarded, and it serves only a local or special interest. There are never any Congressional hearings.

One of the more famous examples of pork was the Big Dig in Boston. This was a 3.5-mile section of highway that was relocated underground, and former House Speaker Thomas "Tip" O'Neill gets credit for bringing that huge chunk of bacon home to his constituents. The project began in 1982 with a budget of $2.8 billion. It took twenty-five years to complete it at a total cost of $14.6 billion. Local contractors gorged themselves at that trough.

Another great example of frivolous pork was the proposed Bridge to Nowhere in Ketchikan, Alaska. This $400 million project proposed building a bridge from Ketchikan to Gravina Island, which had a small international airport but only fifty residents. The bridge would pave the way for a private contractor to build a for-profit prison on the island. But local officials rejected the idea, and the bridge was never built; however, the state still got $300 million in transportation funds.

In 2021, Nancy Pelosi managed to secure $200 million for a park in her San Francisco district. The park, known as the Presidio, is located on the tip of the San Francisco Peninsula within view of the Golden Gate Bridge. The Presidio Trust, a board that oversees the national park, has been trying for years to raise the $200 million needed to restore a thirty-acre section of the park called Fort Scott, which includes twenty historic buildings built more than a hundred years ago as a military installation to protect the San Francisco Bay. Pelosi set aside a $200 million handout to the park, even though the trust acknowledges on its website that it was "charged with operating the park without taxpayer support."

While Democrats supported Pelosi's earmark, Republicans cried foul, noting that members of the Presidio Trust contributed $19 million to Pelosi and the Democratic Congressional Campaign Committee, including a $1 million contribution made just three months before the $200 million handout was included in the House reconciliation budget.

One of the harshest critics of earmarks and pork barrel was late Arizona Sen. John McCain. McCain thought they were flat-out dishonest. Between 2008 and 2010, 51 percent of the earmarks and 61 percent of all earmark money went to only 15 percent of the members of Congress—the eighty-one members of the House and Senate Appropriations committees. "The more powerful you are, the more likely it is you get the earmark in," McCain said in 2014. "Therefore, it's a corrupt system."

Billions for Museums

Although the House Appropriations Committee enacted a ban on earmarks in 2010, the spending went on anyway. Machiavelli would have been proud to see that kind of deceit; say one thing that sounds honorable, but then keep doing whatever you want to maintain your power. More than $50 million went toward building an indoor rainforest in Iowa. A teapot museum in Sparta, North Carolina got half a million. A quarter of a million dollars went to researchers studying goth culture in Blue Springs, Missouri. Theaters, opera houses, museums, and cultural centers were awarded billions. That's not a typo. Billions.

Since 1991, 111,702 earmarks costing $392.5 billion have been funneled to special interests. In 2021, the 285 earmarks identified by the Citizens Against Government Waste cost us $16.8 billion.

Now, what's really happening here? If you're one of the select few who get on one of the appropriations committees, why, exactly, are you doling out all these Christmas gifts? As an act of goodwill?

When I was in the Mob, we helped build community centers and donated to churches, charities, clubs, and youth centers. This was a Mafia tradition that went all the way back to the Old Country; the Mafia formed in Italy as a way to keep enemies and exploiters at bay, and we continued that legacy in New York City, Chicago, Kansas City, and Las Vegas. Even *The Godfather* celebrated this practice by showing Vito Corleone, played by Marlon Brando, dispensing favors for free. It was a sign of how the don wanted to bind people to him and his family, how he valued loyalty and trust. Of course, not all those favors were free; when the Corleones needed favors, the don's supplicants were expected to deliver.

And that's what's happening with pork and earmarks. These huge financial gifts to the select few are not to create a sense of contentment and security in communities but instead are quid-pro-quo payments to political supporters, bribes to big business, or big-time power plays to fortify a politician's reputation and clout. Tip O'Neill was a classic Democrat; do you think when he brought home the bacon for the Big Dig that he didn't turn around and ask favors of the unions and contractors who benefited from this free-flowing conduit of cash?

House Democrats reinstated earmarks in 2021. For-profit entities are still banned from receiving them, and the Government Accountability Office is planning to audit "a sample" of enacted earmarks and report back to Congress. But it's safe to say the fiscal floodgates have been thrown open once again.

Rand Paul, the Republican from Kentucky and the chairman of the Federal Spending Oversight and Emergency Management Subcommittee, released an annual government waste report in early 2021 that listed some of the more ridiculous things the government spends its money on. For instance, it funded a $1.3 million study to determine whether people will eat ground-up bugs. It paid $36 million to ask why stress makes peoples' hair turn gray. It spent more than $3 million interviewing San Franciscans about their use of edible cannabis. For more than twenty years, Northeastern University researchers got $3 million from the National Institutes of Health to watch hamsters fight. The scientists would inject hamsters with steroids and cocaine and then put them in cages with other hamsters to see if they were more aggressive. Now, what you do with the results of a study like that is beyond me.

Waste at the Pentagon

To find the most egregious example of waste, you really have to look at the Defense Department. The DOD, which is usually referred to as the Pentagon, has an annual budget of more than $700 billion. It gets fifty-four cents out of every dollar in federal appropriations. That sounds like a lot, but when you look at the price gouging the DOD deals with from its own defense contractors, you can see that they need every penny of it.

Defense contractors have doled out about $267 million in

campaign contributions to both Democrats and Republicans. Their annual contributions have quintupled since 1990, from about $7.7 million a year to nearly $35 million in 2020. In addition, they spend millions more to lobby Congress. As a result, they have secured legislation that allows them to lock in prices and corner the market. Market forces and competition usually drive prices down as competing companies look for ways to keep their prices lower than everyone else in the market. But since defense contractors often have a monopoly, they can charge whatever they want.

Consider military parts. A company called TransDigm is the sole source of parts for the military, and in 2019, they made headlines by overcharging the government by as much as 4,451 percent for certain items. For instance, an F-15 jet lug that costs $3 to make is sold to the government for $67. A $369 valve assembly pump goes for $8,819. These were not isolated incidents. According to legal scholar Charles Tiefer of the University of Baltimore School of Law, the Pentagon is looking at a $91 million bill in coming years for parts valued at $28 million. This is from a company that has been awarded $500 million in grants from the government over the last five years.

There was nothing illegal about what TransDigm did. In fact, that kind of gouging goes on all the time. They didn't even violate Department of Defense rules. The only mistake TransDigm made was to let the media catch wind of their underhanded tricks. It all came out on a slow news day when the media happened to attend hearings in which Republican Sen. Chuck Grassley and Democratic Rep. Alexandria Ocasio-Cortez raked TransDigm over the coals.

Meanwhile, defense contractors continue to flood Congress with timely political donations. In return, they get to keep the monopolies that allow them to charge exorbitant prices. The contractors even got Congress to pass a law in 2016 that locks in prices; once the Pentagon pays an exorbitant price for an item, they have to keep on paying it.

And while Congress is bending over for the defense contractors, the Department of Defense cooks its own books to hide the truth. Since 1990, all departments and agencies in the federal government have been required to conduct annual audits. Everyone else complied, but the Pentagon blew it off. Finally, Congress ordered a third party to do the audit.

That didn't work either. The auditors came back to Congress and said they couldn't complete the job. The Pentagon's books were so corroded with errors, bookkeeping deficiencies, and outright disregard for factual accounting that the auditors said an audit was impossible.

According to an investigation by the *Nation*, the Pentagon dreamed up trillions of dollars of nonexistent transactions to justify its budgets to Congress. What's more, when the DOD gets funds from Congress, it moves them around however it wants, socking away unspent funds that are supposed to go back into the federal budget (a process called "plugging") or simply shifting money from its congressionally authorized purpose to a different purpose, sometimes over and over again in a way that makes the money impossible to trace. All of this violates Article I, Section 9 of the US Constitution.

But, from a criminal standpoint, it's a thing of beauty, right? I mean these Pentagon bosses are brilliant. They do what they want, thumb their noses at Congress, and spend money as they choose. In 2015, for instance, Congress appropriated $122 billion to the Army. But thanks to the DOD's fuck-you-Mr.-Auditor bookkeeping, the Army's budget included an additional $6.5 trillion in plugs. One Pentagon whistleblower estimated the DOD has stashed as much as $100 billion. I don't know about you, but this makes me think of Tony Soprano stashing cash in the birdseed or in his garage floor.

And they've been getting away with it for years. Back in the 1980s, the Pentagon routinely overestimated inflation rates for weapons systems, according to the whistleblower Franklin "Chuck" Spinney. They never returned the excess funds to the treasury and instead built up a slush fund to use for off-the-books missions. When a team of researchers from Michigan State University cracked open the Pentagon's books in 2017, they discovered that the same year the Army got its $122 billion budget, it also received a cash deposit from the US Treasury for $794.8 billion. This was not an anomaly either. Looking at records back to 1998, the Michigan State team found that the amount of money flowing into and out of the Pentagon was vastly higher than their Congressional budgets. We're talking $1.7 trillion in 1998, $2.3 trillion the next year, $1.7 trillion in 2012, and so on. From 1998 to 2015, $21 trillion—very nearly the amount of our national debt—could not be traced, documented, or explained, Michigan State said.

Despite these well-known and publicly reported shenanigans, Congress continues to increase the Pentagon's budget each year. The $716 billion it got in 2019 was $24 billion more than the year before, which was $6 billion more than the year before that. The US spends more on its military than the next ten highest-spending countries combined. And according to the *Nation* investigation, "No one knows for sure how the biggest single-line item in the US federal budget is actually being spent."

Listen, I'm in favor of a strong military. And no one is saying that $21 trillion that went unaccounted for was misused or misappropriated. All we can say for sure is that one place where most of our tax dollars go does a terrible job of ensuring the money is being responsibly spent. Even Donald Rumsfeld, the secretary of defense under Bush in 2001, admitted there was a problem. He said in a 2001 press conference that the Pentagon couldn't track $2.3 trillion in transactions. He didn't know whether funding went to the intended programs. He didn't know what things actually cost. He didn't know whether payments were going to correct accounts. If this situation existed in private industry, people would go to jail.

Rumsfeld's conclusion? The United States' number one enemy wasn't Russia or even China.

"It's the Pentagon bureaucracy," he concluded. It's not the fighting men and women, but the dishonest bureaucrats. They need to be held accountable. We go to jail for these things. The IRS prosecutes us for tax evasion, and yet the money we pay is used and abused and NOTHING happens.

Rumsfeld's declaration about the Pentagon's missing $2.3 trillion was big news, but the next day brought bigger news: the September 11 terrorist attacks. Suddenly, no one really wanted to talk about how the Pentagon was wasting money. The discussion turned to what we needed to give our military to wage a global war on terrorism.

Conclusion

"We the people are the rightful masters of both Congress and the Courts, not to overthrow the Constitution but to overthrow the men who would pervert the Constitution."

—ABRAHAM LINCOLN

IN THE YEARS FOLLOWING THE GREAT RECESSION OF 2008, I made scores of trips around the country as a public speaker. I spoke with thousands of people in large and small cities from the West Coast to the East Coast and many, many places in between. In every setting, people told me how disillusioned they are about their government and elected leaders. People felt forgotten, ignored, and taken for granted. Many of them suggested that the Mob would do a better job running their country than the leaders they elected.

Unfortunately, that would not be the cure our country needs. While it's true that the Mafia at times exhibits more loyalty, ingenuity, and ambition than our government, let's not lose sight of the fact that the business of organized crime is often based on threats, coercion, bribes, theft, and extortion. That's not a recipe for democratic success, and as I've documented in this book, we're already seeing what happens when our elected leaders adopt the practices of everyday criminals.

Our politicians have taken what was intended by our forefathers to be "This Thing of Yours"—a system of representative government—and turned it into "This Thing of Ours"—the translation of La Cosa Nostra. As in organized crime, our government today is used primarily for the personal advantage of those who run it.

And it is straight out of Machiavelli, the philosophy that fuels the hearts, minds, and attitude of the Mob. Listen, I didn't join the Mafia out of a sense of brotherhood. I joined to make money and to try and get my father out of the rotting prison cell he was in. I didn't join to enjoy an easy life. I knew it would be hard, and it was, but that was the trade-off I was willing to make to earn the millions I needed to help my dad. The money I siphoned away from the government is a drop in the bucket compared to the amount of hard-earned taxpayer money our government officials routinely waste and use for their own personal gain.

Few people enter politics out of a sense of altruism. Mostly they run (and put up with indignity of public scrutiny, endure mudslinging by their opponents, and make humiliating appeals for money from influential lobbyists) to capitalize on the office. They don't run to pass laws to help their constituents. They run to do the bidding of lobbyists and campaign contributors who need the government's help in bolstering their bottom line.

If all of this sounds cynical to you, then you need to go back and reread a few chapters in this book because it's all laid out there for you in black and white. If you're a taxpayer in this country, you are getting fleeced. You might not realize it, but you are witnessing the transformation of our government where the red, white, and blue stripes of Uncle Sam are morphing into the black and white pinstripes of *The Godfather.*

A Crumbling Code

Our government resembles the Mob in the way politicians behave but also in the way it is steadily decaying. The Mob had already begun to crumble by the time Rudy Giuliani came along with his RICO cases. The Mafia was built on *omerta*, the code of silence and honor that compelled people like my father to spend decades in prison rather than rat out his fellow criminals. But that code was losing its grip as mobsters like John Gotti, Paul Castellano, and Joe Bonanno were much more open about their criminal behavior and violated our code again and again. Rudy and RICO were just the strong wind that blew down the house of cards the Mob had become. It had already begun to crumble from the inside.

I see similarities with what's happening in our government right now. There is a growing disrespect for the code of honor that once came with holding elected office. Today, politicians have no qualms about using their office for personal gain. As I've documented again and again in this book, they openly and remorselessly deceive us with impunity.

Even as I write the conclusion for this book, President Joe Biden and his decision to remove troops from Afghanistan are demonstrating how much our country's integrity has crumbled. Despite Biden's promise to Americans that the Taliban would never take over Afghanistan, the rebels waltzed into one city after another just days after the last evacuation helicopter lifted off. After twenty years and a trillion dollars in resources dedicated to driving out the terrorists who attacked us on 9/11, we fled the country in utter disgrace.

What's more, the evacuation itself was tragically amateurish. We left American citizens behind to fend for themselves. We deserted the allies who stood by us for two decades. Biden was supposed to be the "steady hand" our country needed, but the US looked as foolish during this evacuation as it did almost fifty years ago when it abandoned South Vietnam and ended the Vietnam War. Even Biden's supporters agreed the chaotic Afghan withdrawal was, as the *Daily Beast* reported, "one of the greater missteps of the War on Terror." Biden knew the Taliban was in a position to bum-rush the country, but he ardently denied it again and again prior to the withdrawal. Maybe that's why the US left behind tens of millions of dollars worth of vehicles, equipment, and aircraft when it fled Kabul.

Of course, the real victims of Biden's botched withdrawal are the women and girls of Afghanistan. The Taliban don't hold them in the same high regard as we do, and all the gains Afghan women enjoyed in the last twenty years are likely to be wiped out under the Taliban regime. Women will be required to cover their faces in public, leave their jobs, abandon their schools, and accept forced marriage. We can only pray that the public flogging and executions won't be brought back.

People like to blame Donald Trump for the insurrection at the Capitol in the wake of the 2020 presidential election, but I see that incident as the culmination of our nation's frustration over the lying and deceit they hear every time any politician opens their mouth. If Americans can't agree on what we want to be as a nation, it's because our political leaders can't agree and their mutual hatred is trickling down to the rest of us.

And why are politicians on both sides entrenched in this warfare? Simple. It's money. It's all about money and power. The money in politics coats everything in a kind of suffocating slime. You can't *be* in politics unless you're willing to devote yourself to constantly raising money, and the tried-and-true method for raising money is to show that you are fighting a villain. For Democrats, the villain is the Republican Party. For the Republicans, it's the Democratic Party. In a world corrupted by money, your only option is to raise more than your opponent. It's as simple as that, folks.

When raising money is the sole measure of success, politicians will do anything. They'll restrict voting rights. They'll redraw districts so that even if they are in a minority in a state they can win most of the elections, which is what happened in Pennsylvania in 2012 when Republicans got only 49 percent of the vote in House races but managed to win thirteen of the state's eighteen House seats. That's a rigged system.

Solving the Problem

What are the answers? I'm not a policymaker, but you don't need to be a political or social scientist to see the big problems and the big solutions. For starters, couldn't our elected officials honor their own code of conduct as strictly as the Mafia ONCE honored its code of *omerta?* Could this aspect of the Mafia serve as an example for our politicians? Novelist Kurt Vonnegut thought so. "There is no reason why good cannot triumph as often as evil," Vonnegut once said. "The triumph of anything is a matter of organization. If there are such things as angels, I hope that they are organized along the lines of the Mafia."

Until that happens, here are some other things we can do:

- **We've got to make it easier for people to vote, and we have to protect everyone's right to vote.** We've got to blow the whistle when states like Florida try to restrict our right to vote. In 2018, Florida voters overwhelmingly supported restoring voting rights to ex-felons. But even before a vote could be cast, the state legislature took those rights away. As an ex-felon, that angered me, and now I'm watching places like Georgia making it harder for regular citizens to vote when we should be encouraging *all* people to vote.

- **We've got to reform the campaign finance system.** The election in 2020 was the costliest in US history, and most of the spending came from a small cluster of really rich people who could afford to donate huge sums. As this book points out, those contributors flex incredible muscle within our political system and send the average voter to the back of the line. Our issues never get heard. What's worse, the high cost of running for office often keeps women and candidates of color out because they don't have the wealthy financial connections white candidates have.

- **We need term limits.** Politics was never supposed to be a career, but now we have politicians who enter Congress as average citizens and leave as millionaires thirty years later. We continue to let this happen. Let's set some limits so campaign funders have less incentive to invest in someone who's going to be gone in just a few years.

- **We need to send lawmakers to jail when they use insider knowledge to get rich.** At the very least, let's require all elected officials to put their investments into blind trusts while they are in office.

- **Lock the revolving door.** By that, I mean let's ban elected leaders from becoming lobbyists. This is a no-brainer, people. It cuts the incentive of politicians to give political favors in return for a lucrative job after they leave office. More than half of former Congress people leave office for high-paid lobbying jobs.

- **Let's pass a law that any corporation that does business** with the federal government has to disclose how much they spend to influence elections. Let's make it easy to connect the dots so we can identify those who are rigging the system.

- **We've got to find a way to get average citizens a voice in Washington.** Right now, 94 percent of the interest groups in DC represent executives and professionals. What about the carpenters and the plumbers and the artists and the environmentalists? What about the Uber drivers? I like a solution proposed by Archon Fung, the Winthrop Laflin McCormack professor of citizenship and self-government at the Harvard Kennedy School. He supports a system where every American gets a five-hundred-dollar voucher to spend each year on a lobbyist of their choice. "Suppose your pet issue is combating climate change or banning abortion," Fung says. "If you found sixty other people with similar interests, you could pool your vouchers to hire an organizer and pay him or her a thirty-thousand-dollar salary to help you lobby for your cause."

- **Cut defense spending immediately, and continue cutting it by 10 percent a year until an outside, third-party special commission has straightened out the military's books.** The Department of Defense is a black hole that swallows half of our tax dollars, and we have no accounting whatsoever for how it spends its money. While we're at it, let's roll back any law that allows defense contractors to have a monopoly and protections from price gouging. We spend way more on the military than all the other superpowers in the world combined. Meanwhile, our roads crumble.

- **Each of us should be able to designate the first two hundred dollars of our tax payments to support the political candidate of our choice.** This is former White House lawyer Richard Painter's idea. He calls it a "tax rebate for democracy" and says it would generate billions in small donations to candidates and remove the need for those candidates to accept money from that tiny slice of wealthy individuals and corporations who want to pull all the strings on our government.?

In addition, we need to ban earmarks and pork-barrel legislation, provide incentives for government agencies to save money, stop using government "public affairs" offices to promote propaganda, and empower a commission with clout that is authorized to clean up the labyrinth of overlapping and archaic rules and regulations in the federal code.

I'm in favor of dramatically reducing the size of the federal bureaucracy, but if there is one agency I'd like to see strengthened, it's the Office of Information and Regulatory Affairs—the outfit that measures the costs and benefits of federal regulations. They have fewer than fifty people reviewing measures being written by tens of thousands of agency regulators. They are outgunned. Let's give them some ammunition to stem the torrent of federal regulations that fuel our country's crony capitalism and put shackles on our entrepreneurs.

I have to be honest. When I was first approached about writing this book, I felt strongly that our government was operating like the Mob. I knew our politicians were two-faced, that our regulations were crippling, and that our spending was out of control. But as I started to do the research, I realized that the problems were far worse than I had imagined.

This is a big job, folks. There is a lot to do. I'm not naive enough to think some of the problems I've highlighted in this book can be dealt with easily. But the first step is for all of us to be aware of what's going on and let our elected leaders know that we've had enough.

As I have throughout this book, I've turned to our great leaders and prominent thinkers to find the words that will inspire us to act. There are a lot to choose from, but the best ones, in my mind, focus on the importance of what individuals can do to reform politics and an oppressive government. For instance, Margaret Mead once said, "Never doubt that a small group of thoughtful, committed citizens can change the world. Indeed, it is the only thing that ever has." Dwight Eisenhower said, "Politics ought to be the part-time profession of every citizen who would protect the rights and privileges of free men."

But maybe the best call to action came from eighteenth-century Irish philosopher and statesman Edmund Burke, who strongly criticized Great Britain's treatment of its American colonies.

"Nobody," Burke said, "makes a greater mistake than he who does nothing because he could do only a little."

Resources

Below are some of the books and articles I used when researching this book.

Introduction

Gordon, Noah J. "How Did Members of Congress Get So Wealthy?" *The Atlantic*, September 9, 2014. https://www.theatlantic.com/politics/archive/2014/09/how-did-members-of-congress-get-so-wealthy/379848/

Schweizer, Peter. *Throw Them All Out: How Politicians and Their Friends Get Rich Off Insider Stock Tips, Land Deals, and Cronyism That Would Send the Rest of Us to Prison.* Boston: Houghton Mifflin Harcourt, 2011.

Charen, Mona. "News of Over-Regulation Reaches the *New York Times*." *National Review*, December 29, 2017. https://www.nationalreview.com/2017/12/over-regulation-hurts-united-states-economy-new-york-times-report/

Chapter 1

Staff. "The Mafia Today." *The Week*, April 21, 2019. https://theweek.com/articles/835970/mafia-today

Editors. "SparkNotes: The Prince." SparkNotes. 2022. https://www.sparknotes.com/philosophy/prince/context/#:~:text=Machiavelli%20desperately%20wanted%20to%20return,position%20within%20the%20Florentine%20government

McCreesh, Shawn. "Is the American Mafia on the Rise?" *Rolling Stone,* November 22, 2016. https://www.rollingstone.com/culture/culture-features/is-the-american-mafia-on-the-rise-108421/

Editors. "Origins of the Mafia." History.com. May 28, 2019. https://www.history.com/topics/crime/origins-of-the-mafia

"The New Mafia is Deadlier." *New York Times,* January 12, 1964. https://www.nytimes.com/1964/01/12/archives/the-new-mafia-is-deadlier-the-old-sicilian-gangsters-had-a-rural.html

Raab, Selwyn. *Five Families: The Rise, Decline, and Resurgence of America's Most Powerful Mafia Empires.* New York: St. Martin's Publishing Group, 2016.

Bissell, Tim. "When Mussolini's Mafia Buster Cleaned Up Sicily—and Sent Mobsters to America." Ozy.com. January 17, 2018. https://www.ozy.com/true-and-stories/when-mussolinis-mafia-buster-cleaned-up-sicily-and-sent-mobsters-to-america/83026/

Williams, Owen. "Mussolini vs the Mafia." HistoryAnswers.co.uk. August 9, 2019. https://www.historyanswers.co.uk/people-politics/mussolini-vs-the-mafia/

Bonanno, Joseph. *A Man of Honor: The Autobiography of Joseph Bonanno.* New York: St. Martin's Publishing Group, 2003.

Jacobs, James B., and Ellen Peters. "Labor Racketeering: The Mafia and the Unions." *Crime and Justice.* Vol. 30, *A Review of Research,* edited by Michael Tonry. Chicago: University of Chicago Press, 2003. https://doi.org/10.1086/652232

Kimeldorf, Howard. *Reds or Rackets?* Berkeley: University of California Press, 1988.

Silverman, Ira, and Alan A. Block. "On the Lam with an Uber-Mobster." *New Yorker,* November 6, 1994. https://www.newyorker.com/magazine/1994/11/14/on-the-lam-with-an-uber-mobster

Luckhurst, Toby. "The New York Mafia: What's Happening to the Five Families?" BBC News online. March 14, 2019. https://www.bbc.com/news/world-us-canada-47566981

Arnold, Amanda. "A 24-Year-Old Is Accused of Killing a Mob Boss. It Gets Weirder From There." *New York,* July 22, 2019. https://www.thecut.com/2019/07/gambino-mob-boss-frank-cali-killing-everything-we-know.html

Chapter 2

Drutman, Lee. "A Better Way to Fix Lobbying." Brookings. *Issues in Governance Studies,* no. 40 (June 2011). https://www.brookings.edu/wp-content/uploads/2016/06/06_lobbying_drutman.pdf

Hill, Charlotte. "America's Lobbying System is Broken." *HuffPost*, June 7, 2017. https://www.
huffpost.com/entry/americas-lobbying-system-is-broken_b_5938a0cfe4b014ae8c69dd90

Sobel, Russell S., and J.R. Clark. "Interest Group Activity and Government Growth: A Causality
Analysis." Cato Institute. *Cato Journal*. Vol. 36, no. 3 (2016). http://faculty.citadel.edu/sobel/
All%20Pubs%20PDF/Interest%20Group%20Activity%20and%20Government%20Growth.pdf

Berman, Russell. "An Exodus From Congress Tests the Lure of Lobbying." *The
Atlantic*, May 1, 2018. https://www.theatlantic.com/politics/archive/2018/05/
lobbying-the-job-of-choice-for-retired-members-of-congress/558851/

Williamson, Elizabeth. "Getting Around Rules on Lobbying." *Washington Post,* October 14, 2007.

Craig, John, and David Madland. "How Campaign Contributions and Lobbying Can
Lead to Inefficient Economic Policy." Center for American Progress. May 2, 2014.
https://www.americanprogress.org/issues/economy/reports/2014/05/02/88917/
how-campaign-contributions-and-lobbying-can-lead-to-inefficient-economic-policy/

Drutman, Lee. "How Corporate Lobbyists Conquered American Democracy." *The Atlantic*, April
20, 2015.

Williamson, Elizabeth. "Industries Paid for Top Regulators' Travel." *Washington Post,* November
2, 2007.

Waterhouse, Benjamin C. *Lobbying America: The Politics of Business from Nixon to NAFTA.*
Princeton, NJ: Princeton University Press, 2013.

Lindsey, Brink, and Steven Teles. *The Captured Economy.* Oxford: Oxford University Press, 2017.

Mayer, Lloyd Hitoshi. "What Is This 'Lobbying' That We Are So Worried About?" Notre Dame
Law School. *Yale Law & Policy Review* 26, no. 485 (2008).

Senate Office of Public Records. "Total lobbying spending in the United States from 1998 to
2020." OpenSecrets. 2022. https://www.opensecrets.org/federal-lobbying

Powell, Lewis F., Jr. to Eugene B. Sydnor, Jr. Memorandum. "Attack on American Free Enterprise
System." Scholarly Commons, Washington and Lee University School of Law, 1971. https://
scholarlycommons.law.wlu.edu/powellmemo/

Drutman, Lee. *The Business of America is Lobbying: How Corporations Became Politicized and
Politics Became More Corporate.* Oxford: Oxford University Press, 2015.

Kliff, Sarah. "Obamacare Repeal Would Cost Insurers $1 Trillion." *Washington Post,* May 2012.
https://www.washingtonpost.com/blogs/wonkblog/post/obamacare-repeal-would-cost-
insurers-1-trillion/2012/05/15/gIQADGbrRU_blog.html?utm_term=.9071dd2679ac

Lipton, Eric, and Kenneth Vogel. "Progressives Press Biden to Limit Corporate Influence in Administration." *New York Times*, November 12, 2020.

Chapter 3

Editors. "The King Of Frauds: How the Credit Mobilier Bought Its Way Through Congress." *The Sun*, September 4, 1872.

Sitkoff, Robert H. "Politics and the Business Corporation." Harvard University. *Regulation* 26 (Winter 2003–2004). https://papers.ssrn.com/sol3/papers.cfm?abstract_id=479821

Painter, Richard. *Taxation Only With Representation*. Auburn, AL: Take Back Our Republic, 2016.

"Campaign Finance and American Democracy." University of Toronto. *Annual Review of Political Science* 18 (May 2015). https://doi.org/10.1146/annurev-polisci-010814-104523

Koerth, Maggie. "How Money Affects Elections." *FiveThirtyEight*, September 2018. https://fivethirtyeight.com/features/money-and-elections-a-complicated-love-story/

La Raja, Raymond J., and Brian F. Schaffner. *Campaign Finance and Political Polarization: When Purists Prevail*. Ann Arbor: University of Michigan Press, 2015. Painter,

Richard W. "The Conservative Case for Campaign-Finance Reform." *New York Times*, February 3, 2016. https://www.nytimes.com/2016/02/03/opinion/the-conservative-case-forcampaign-finance-reform.html

Jones, Bradley. "Most Americans Want to Limit Campaign Spending, Say Big Donors Have Greater Political Influence." Pew Research Center. May 8, 2018. https://www.pewresearch.org/fact-tank/2018/05/08/most-americans-want-to-limit-campaign-spending-say-big-donors-have-greater-political-influence/

Seitz-Wald, Alex. "Democrats Used to Rail against 'Dark Money.' Now They're Better at it than the GOP." NBC News online. September 13, 2020. https://www.nbcnews.com/politics/2020-election/democrats-used-rail-against-dark-money-now-they-re-better-n1239830

Cummings, Jeanne. "New Dem Money Group Takes On GOP." *Politico*, April 29, 2011. https://www.politico.com/story/2011/04/new-dem-money-group-takes-on-gop-053905

Federal Election Commission. "2016 Outside Spending, by Group." OpenSecrets. 2022. https://www.opensecrets.org/outsidespending/summ.php?cycle=2016&chrt=V&disp=O&type=U

Content First, LLC Editors. "Foreign Direct Investment in the United States 2020." Global Business Alliance. August 2020. https://canaz.net/wp-content/uploads/2020/09/FDIUS-2020-Report.pdf

Lipton, Eric, Brooke Williams, and Nicholas Confessore. "Foreign Powers Buy Influence at Think Tanks." *New York Times,* September 6, 2014. https://www.nytimes.com/2014/09/07/us/politics/foreign-powers-buy-influence-at-think-tanks.html

Bjørgaas, Tove. "Norway's Role in Foreign Policy Research and Implementation in the United States." Norwegian Peacebuilding Resource Centre. May 2012. https://www.documentcloud.org/documents/1284105-1-aaa-general-doc-viewer_new.html#document/p5/a176108

Chapter 4

"Richard Burr, Estimated Net Worth 2008–2018." OpenSecrets. 2022. https://www.opensecrets.org/personal-finances/net-worth?cid=N00002221

Faturechi, Robert, and Derek Willis. "On the Same Day Sen. Richard Burr Dumped Stock, So Did His Brother-in-Law. Then the Market Crashed." *ProPublica,* May 6, 2020. https://www.propublica.org/article/burr-family-stock

Lipton, Eric, and Nicholas Fandos. "Senator Richard Burr Sold a Fortune in Stocks as G.O.P. Played Down Coronavirus Threat." *New York Times,* May 14, 2020. https://www.nytimes.com/2020/03/19/us/politics/richard-burr-stocks-sold-coronavirus.html

Faturechi, Robert. "Senate Intel Chair Sold Dutch Fertilizer Stock in 2018, Right Before a Collapse." *ProPublica,* April 7, 2020. https://www.propublica.org/article/senate-intel-chair-sold-dutch-fertilizer-stock-in-2018-right-before-a-collapse

Keating, Dan, Scott Higham, Kimberly Kindy, and David S. Fallis. "Capitol Assets: Congress's Wealthiest Mostly Shielded in Deep Recession." *Washington Post,* October 6, 2012. https://www.washingtonpost.com/investigations/capitol-assets-congresss-wealthiest-mostly-shielded-in-deep-recession/2012/10/06/5a70605c-102f-11e2-acc1-e927767f41cd_story.html

Mui, Ylan Q. "Americans Saw Wealth Plummet 40 Percent from 2007 to 2010, Federal Reserve Says." *Washington Post,* June 11, 2012. https://www.washingtonpost.com/business/economy/fed-americans-wealth-dropped-40-percent/2012/06/11/gJQAllsCVV_story.html?tid=a_inl_manual

Kotch, Alex. "Revealed: How US Senators Invest in Firms They Are Supposed to Regulate." *The Guardian,* September 19, 2019. https://www.theguardian.com/us-news/2019/sep/19/us-senators-investments-conflict-of-interest

Tahoun, Ahmed, and Laurence van Lent. "The Personal Wealth Interests of Politicians and Government Intervention in the Economy." Oxford University. *Review of Finance* 23, no. 1, February 2019. https://doi.org/10.1093/rof/rfy015

Pisani, Bob. "Why Warren Buffett's Way of Beating the Market Will Not Be Easily Repeated." CNBC online. September 22, 2020. https://www.cnbc.com/2020/09/22/why-warren-buffets-way-of-beating-the-market-will-not-be-repeated.html

Schwartz, John. "Not-So-Representative Investors." *New York Times,* July 9, 2011. https://www.nytimes.com/2011/07/10/business/mutfund/congressional-portfolios-outpacing-the-market-essay.html

Kindy, Kimberly, David Fallis, and Scott Higham. "Congress Members Back Legislation That Could Benefit Themselves, Relatives." *Washington Post,* October 7, 2012. https://www.washingtonpost.com/politics/congress-members-back-legislation-that-could-benefit-themselves-relatives/2012/10/07/c2fa7d94-f3a9-11e1-a612-3cfc842a6d89_story.html

Gongloff, Mark. "Stock Act Change Just Quietly Made It Easier for Top Federal Employees to Inside Trade." *HuffPost,* April 17, 2013. https://www.huffpost.com/entry/stock-act-change-insider-trading_n_3100115

Chapter 5

Crain, Nicole V., and W. Mark Crain. *The Impact of Regulatory Costs on Small Firms.* Washington, DC: SBA Office of Advocacy, September 2010.

Editors. "Over-Regulated America." *The Economist,* February 18, 2012. https://www.economist.com/leaders/2012/02/18/over-regulated-america

Xu, Tanya. "Regulations Could Be Increasing Consumer Prices." *Regulatory Review,* September 29, 2016. https://www.theregreview.org/2016/09/29/xu-regulations-could-be-increasing-consumer-prices/

Teles, Steven M. "Kludgeocracy in America." *National Affairs,* Fall 2013. https://www.nationalaffairs.com/publications/detail/kludgeocracy-in-america

Leonhardt, Megan. "Economist: The System Is Flawed When Most Americans Have Little or No Retirement Savings." CNBC online. December 12, 2019. https://www.cnbc.com/2019/12/12/system-is-flawed-when-most-americans-have-tiny-retirement-savings.html

Editors. "Too Much Federal Regulation Has Piled Up in America." *The Economist,* March 2, 2017. https://www.economist.com/united-states/2017/03/02/too-much-federal-regulation-has-piled-up-in-america

Zajac, Andrew. "Regulators Surge in Numbers While Overseers Shrink." *Washington Post,* June 24, 2012. https://www.washingtonpost.com/business/economy/regulators-surge-in-numbers-while-overseers-shrink/2012/06/24/gJQArWvDoV_story.html

Ellig, Jerry, and Richard Williams. "David versus Godzilla: Bigger Stones." Penn State Dickinson Law. *Dickinson Law Review* 125, no. 1, Fall 2020. https://ideas.dickinsonlaw.psu.edu/cgi/viewcontent.cgi?article=1102&context=dlr

Batkins, Sam. "Deregulation Under Obama and Trump." American Action Forum. June 28, 2107. https://www.americanactionforum.org/insight/deregulation-obama-trump/

Laffer, William. "How Regulation Is Destroying American Jobs." The Heritage Foundation. February 16, 1993. https://www.heritage.org/government-regulation/report/how-regulation-destroying-american-jobs#:~:text=Many%20regulations%20directly%20increase%20the,primary%20engines%20of%20job%20creation

Millsap, Adam A. "How Too Much Regulation Hurts America's Poor." *Forbes,* June 23, 2019. https://www.forbes.com/sites/adammillsap/2019/07/23/how-too-much-regulation-hurts-americas-poor/?sh=32ed1a2c271f

Somin, Ilya. "Moving Vans More Powerful Than Ballot Boxes." *USA Today,* October 18, 2016. https://www.usatoday.com/story/opinion/2016/10/18/mobility-zoning-licensing-voting-minorities-column/91990486/

Glaeser, Edward. "Reforming Land Use Regulations." Brookings. April 24, 2017. https://www.brookings.edu/research/reforming-land-use-regulations/amp/

Chapter 6

Cohn, Jonathan. "What Jon Gruber's Quotes Really Tell Us about Obamacare—and American Politics." *The New Republic,* November 17, 2014. https://newrepublic.com/article/120311/jonathan-gruber-and-obamacare-what-his-quotes-really-tell-us

House Committee on Oversight and Government Reform. *Analysis of the First Year of the Obama Administration: Public Relations and Propaganda Initiatives.* US House of Representatives. 2010. https://republicans-oversight.house.gov/wp-content/uploads/2012/02/8-16-2010_Propaganda_Report.pdf

Gruber, Jonathan. "Getting the Facts Straight on Health Care Reform." *New England Journal of Medicine,* December 2, 2009. https://www.nejm.org/doi/full/10.1056/NEJMp0911715

Thiessen, Marc A. "Thanks to Jonathan Gruber for Revealing Obamacare Deception." *Washington Post,* November 2014. https://www.washingtonpost.com/opinions/marc-thiessen-thanks-to-jonathan-gruber-for-revealing-obamacare-deception/2014/11/17/356514b2-6e72-11e4-893f-86bd390a3340_story.html

Cunningham, Paige Winfield. "Was Gruber the 'Architect' of Obamacare?" *Politico*, November 13, 2014. https://www.politico.com/story/2014/11/obamacare-jonathan-gruber-architect-112886

Hamilton, John Maxwell, and Kevin R. Kosar. "Government Information and Propaganda: How to Draw a Line." LSU Manship School of Mass Communication. *R Street Policy Study* 73 (October 2016). https://www.rstreet.org/wp-content/uploads/2016/11/73.pdf

Hamilton, John Maxwell, and Kevin R. Kosar. "How the American Government Is Trying to Control How You Think." *Washington Post*, September 2015. https://www.washingtonpost.com/posteverything/wp/2015/09/24/the-new-propaganda-how-the-american-government-is-trying-to-control-what-you-think/

Hamilton, John Maxwell. *Manipulating the Masses: Woodrow Wilson and the Birth of American Propaganda*. Baton Rouge: LSU Press, 2020.

Johnson, Carla. "Obamacare National Marketing Campaign to Cost Nearly $700 Million." RealClearPolitics. July 25, 2013. https://www.realclearpolitics.com/articles/2013/07/25/obamacare_national_marketing_campaign_to_cost_nearly_700_million_119368.html

Hamilton, John Maxwell, and Kevin R. Kosar. "Call It What It Is: Propaganda." *Politico*, October 8, 2020. https://www.politico.com/news/magazine/2020/10/08/government-communication-propaganda-427290

Chapter 7

Dincer, Oguzhan, and Michael Johnston. "Measuring Illegal and Legal Corruption in American States: Some Results from the Corruption in America Survey."

Edmond J. Safra Center for Ethics. December 1, 2014. https://ethics.harvard.edu/blog/measuring-illegal-and-legal-corruption-american-states-some-results-safra

Divounguy, Orphe, and Bryce Hill. *Corruption Costs Illinois Taxpayers at Least $550 Million per Year*. Chicago: Illinois Policy Institute, 2019. https://files.illinoispolicy.org/wp-content/uploads/2020/01/IPI_Corruption-Costs.pdf

Waters, Jim. "Corruption's Perception Is Kentucky's Reality." *Bowling Green Daily News*, September 21, 2019. https://www.bgdailynews.com/opinion/commentary/corruption-s-perception-is-kentucky-s-reality/article_6dd03f08-d545-5487-9910-f2fc43ac46bc.html

Divounguy, Orphe, and Michael Johnston. "Measuring Illegal and Legal Corruption in American States." Edmond J. Safra Center for Ethics. December 1, 2014. https://ethics.harvard.edu/blog/measuring-illegal-and-legal-corruption-american-states-some-results-safra

Chase, John, David Kidwell, and Ray Gibson. "Madigan's Kind of Town." *Chicago Tribune,* January 24, 2010. https://www.chicagotribune.com/news/ct-met-michael-madigan-0124-20100122-story.html

Staff. "2019 First Ever 'Scammy Awards' for Corrupt Politicians." TermLimits. August 12, 2019. https://www.termlimits.com/scammy-awards/

Bresnahan, John. "Waters Ethics Case Debacle Detailed." *Politico,* September 25, 2012. https://www.politico.com/story/2012/09/report-details-waters-ethics-case-debacle-081665

Staff. "Corruption Scandals Led to Harry Reid's Abrupt 'Retirement.'" JudicialWatch. March 30, 2015. https://www.judicialwatch.org/corruption-chronicles/corruption-scandals-led-to-harry-reids-abrupt-retirement/

Chapter 8

"*Washington Journal* Federal Income Recipients." C-SPAN video, 43:21. April 23, 2007. https://www.c-span.org/video/?197123-5/federal-income-recipients

Hill, Fiona. "Public Service and the Federal Government." Brookings. May 27, 2020. https://www.brookings.edu/policy2020/votervital/public-service-and-the-federal-government/

Light, Paul C. "The True Size of Government Is Nearing a Record High." Brookings. October 7, 2020. https://www.brookings.edu/blog/fixgov/2020/10/07/the-true-size-of-government-is-nearing-a-record-high/

DiSalvo, Daniel. "The Trouble with Public Sector Unions." *National Affairs,* Fall 2010. https://www.nationalaffairs.com/publications/detail/the-trouble-with-public-sector-unions

Donahue, John D. *The Warping of Government Work.* Cambridge, MA: Harvard University Press, 2008. https://www.hks.harvard.edu/publications/warping-government-work

Chapter 9

Amadeo, Kimberly. "U.S. Debt to China: How Much Is It, and Why?" The Balance. April 7, 2021. https://www.thebalance.com/u-s-debt-to-china-how-much-does-it-own-3306355

Lindorff, Dave. "Exclusive: The Pentagon's Massive Accounting Fraud Exposed." *The Nation,* November 27, 2018. https://www.thenation.com/article/archive/pentagon-audit-budget-fraud/

Federal Election Commission. "Defense Spending." OpenSecrets. March 21, 2021. https://www.
    opensecrets.org/industries/summary.php?ind=D&recipdetail=A&sortorder=U&cycle=All

Smith, Thomas W., and Adam Andrzejewski. *2020 Annual Report*. OpenTheBooks. 2020. https://
    www.openthebooks.com/assets/1/6/Annual_Report_2020_online_FINAL3.pdf

Smith, Thomas W. "Government Waste Thrives in Darkness." *Galion Inquirer,* January 30, 2021.
    https://www.galioninquirer.com/opinion/61352/government-waste-thrives-in-darkness

Andrzejewski, Adam, and Thomas W. Smith. *The Federal Government's Use-It-Or-Lose-It
    Spending Spree: OpenTheBooks Oversight Report*. OpenTheBooks. August 20, 2020. https://
    www.openthebooks.com/assets/1/6/Use-It-Or-Lose-It_2020_v7.pdf

Richardson, Valerie. "Park or Pork? House Republicans Roast Pelosi over $200 Million for San
    Francisco's Presidio." *Washington Times,* September 2, 2021. https://www.washingtontimes.
    com/news/2021/sep/2/house-republicans-roast-nancy-pelosi-over-200-mill/

Tiefer, Charles. "Congress Is Accepting Price Gouging by Defense Contractors."
    Forbes, August 7, 2019. https://www.forbes.com/sites/charlestiefer/2019/08/07/
    congress-is-accepting-war-profiteering/?sh=583e088f711a

Shutt, Jennifer. "House Appropriators Officially Bring Back Earmarks, Ending
    Ban." *Roll Call,* February 26, 2021. https://rollcall.com/2021/02/26/
    house-appropriators-to-cap-earmarks-at-1-percent-of-topline/

Acknowledgments

For my wife, children, and grandchildren. My concern for their future in America inspired me to write this book.

About the Author

MICHAEL FRANZESE is a former caporegime with the Colombo crime family of New York City. In 1986, *Vanity Fair* named him one of the biggest money earners the Mob had seen since Al Capone. At the age of thirty-five, *Fortune* magazine listed him as number eighteen on its list of the "Fifty Most Wealthy and Powerful Mafia Bosses," just five places behind John Gotti.

At his peak, Michael earned millions in cash every week with brilliant scams on the edge of the legitimate business world. He was involved in several industries, including auto dealerships, construction, financial services, and the sports and entertainment business. After successfully defending himself from multiple indictments, Franzese pled guilty to racketeering charges, accepted a ten-year prison sentence, and publicly walked away from the Mob. He is the only high-ranking official of a major crime family to ever walk away without protective custody and survive.

Michael credits his wife, Camille, with his religious conversion. He is in great demand as a public speaker, sharing his life, experiences, and inspiring messages with church groups, professional and student athletes, and corporate executives across the country.

Mafia Democracy is Michael's fifth book.